PRESENTED

To _____

By _____

Date _____

UNCLE ARTHUR'S®

STORYTIME™

CHILDREN'S TRUE ADVENTURES

Classic Edition

Volume Two

Arthur S. Maxwell

STORYGUIDE™ Section
and Exploring the Story Activities
Cheryl Woolsey Holloway

Produced by
Family Media, Inc.
Washington, D.C.

Distributed to the Trade by Wolgemuth & Hyatt, Publishers, Inc.
1749 Mallory Lane, Suite 110, Brentwood, Tennessee 37027

Printed in United States of America

94 93 92 91 90 89   10 9 8 7 6 5 4 3 2 1

Library of Congress Cataloging-in-Publication Data

Maxwell, Arthur Stanley, 1896-
   Uncle Arthur's storytime.

     Summary: Presents a collection of true stories illustrating the values of honesty, love, faith, respect, compassion, and cooperation. Includes activities which reinforce the lessons learned in each story.
     1. Character sketches—Juvenile literature. 2. Virtues—Juvenile literature. 3. Children—Conduct of life. 4. Children—Religious life. [1. Conduct of life] I. Holloway, Cheryl Woolsey, 1956- . II. Title. III. Title: Uncle Arthur's storytime.
BJ1631.M375 1989b   170'.83   89-23309
ISBN 1-877773-01-8 (v. 1)
ISBN 1-877773-00-X (slipcase: v. 1)

ISBN 1-877773-02-6 (v. 2)

CONTENTS

PART ONE

❖

AN INTRODUCTION

Index of Character Traits 8
How to Use Uncle Arthur's® STORYTIME™ Program... 10
Uncle Arthur and the Search for Stories................... 13

PART TWO

❖

THE STORIES AND
THE EXPLORING THE STORY ACTIVITIES

Seventeen Cowards 17
Ronny, the Rope Climber 27
Kim's Cake 35
The Mysterious Rider... 45
Richard's Rubbish Heap... 57
Nellie's Wish 67
Mike, the Blacksmith's Son 79
Aunt Mary's Remedy.. 89
Alan's Sandwich... 99
Sylvia's Glasses 107

PART THREE

❖

THE STORYGUIDE™ SECTION

Motivating Your Child 118
Extending Your Child's Horizons 124

FOREWORD

Uncle Arthur's®
STORYTIME™ Classic Edition has been written for every caring adult who wants to help children develop positive character traits and Christian values.

The STORYTIME program has been designed with three delightful ingredients:

a. True stories that capture a child's active interest.

b. A discussion and activity section following each story that highlights the fun of exploring the story with your child.

c. A STORYGUIDE™ section that provides helpful information on character development and positive parenting.

Although directed to parents, the STORYTIME program can be easily adapted to the curriculum of any educator or Sunday school teacher who wants to help children build the foundation of good character.

ACKNOWLEDGMENTS

Uncle Arthur's® STORYTIME™ Classic Edition is a true classic in craftsmanship. The Glatcotext Web Hi-Brite text paper provides a rich soft texture that adds distinction to the illustrations. The unmistakable typeface is Cheltenham Light. Originally designed by Bertram G. Goodhue in 1896, it was later developed by Morris Fuller Benton and cast by the American Type Foundry in 1902. Today it is one of the most widely known pure American typefaces.

———

We wish to thank the following for the many hours of professional consultation, direction, and advice in the development and formatting of this special work: H. E. Logue, M.D., president-elect of the Alabama District Branch of the American Psychiatric Association, 1989; Jade K. Carter, Ed.D., professor, University of Alabama in Birmingham, Alabama; Raymond S. Moore, Ed.D., and Dorothy N. Moore, M.A., of the Moore Foundation, Camas, Washington. And we especially thank the Moores for providing the concept of using true stories.

———

We also express appreciation and thanks to the Arthur S. Maxwell estate for their kind cooperation and coordination with the Maxwell heritage; Steven R. Schiffman for original concept contributions; Richard Coffen and Lawrence W. Ragan for providing special resources.

STORYTIME Production: Marketing and Product Director: J. Rivers; Editor: Cheryl Woolsey Holloway; Assistant Editor: Stuart Tyner; Project Development and Creative Director: Gail R. Hunt; Project Development Coordinator: Patricia Lance Fritz; Project Creative Assistant: Linda Anderson McDonald; Project Assistants: Suzanne A. Lukes and Vera Kotanko; Slipcase, Cover, and Book Design: Trousdell Design, Inc.; Composition: Xyvision Electronic Publishing System; Market Research: Message Factors, Inc.; Book Cover Illustration: Christy Sheets Mull; Slipcase Cover Illustration: Mark Stutzman; Illustrations: Mary Bausman, Robert Grace, Robert Grist, Christy Sheets Mull, John Williams, Mark Stutzman.

PART ONE

AN INTRODUCTION

INDEX OF CHARACTER TRAITS

Commitment
Richard's Rubbish Heap 57
Mike, the Blacksmith's Son 79

Compassion
The Mysterious Rider 45
Nellie's Wish 67
Sylvia's Glasses 107

Consideration for Physical Impairment
Sylvia's Glasses 107

Cooperation
Aunt Mary's Remedy 89

Courage
Seventeen Cowards 17
Ronny, the Rope Climber 27
Richard's Rubbish Heap 57
Mike, the Blacksmith's Son 79

Faith
The Mysterious Rider 45

Generosity
Nellie's Wish 67

Goal Setting
Richard's Rubbish Heap 57
Aunt Mary's Remedy 89

Honesty
Ronny, the Rope Climber 27
Alan's Sandwich 99

Humility
Seventeen Cowards 17

Kindness

The Mysterious Rider 45

Nellie's Wish.................................... 67

Love

The Mysterious Rider 45

Obedience

Kim's Cake...................................... 35

Aunt Mary's Remedy 89

Alan's Sandwich 99

Persistence

Richard's Rubbish Heap 57

Mike, the Blacksmith's Son.................. 79

Resisting Peer Pressure

Ronny, the Rope Climber..................... 27

Respect

Seventeen Cowards............................ 17

Kim's Cake...................................... 35

Aunt Mary's Remedy 89

Responsibility

Seventeen Cowards............................ 17

Kim's Cake...................................... 35

Nellie's Wish.................................... 67

Sharing

The Mysterious Rider 45

Nellie's Wish.................................... 67

Teamwork

Aunt Mary's Remedy 89

Tidiness

Aunt Mary's Remedy 89

How to Use
Uncle Arthur's® STORYTIME™
Program

The STORYTIME program is a fun, easy-to-use system for positive character development. It is designed to help parents share with their children positive character traits and Christian values as they read and discuss stories and enjoy family activities together.

The STORYTIME system includes three elements:

1. Simple, true-to-life stories to share with children the traditional values and principles of good character.

2. Exploring the Story. Located at the end of the story, Exploring the Story makes each STORYTIME experience an exciting adventure. Exploring the Story helps parents and children discuss and reinforce the lessons shared in each story through Fun Footnotes, games, simple crafts, and activities designed for three age

levels—preschool, early elementary, and later elementary.

3. Each book also contains a STORYGUIDE ™ section for parents, providing valuable information on character development and child rearing. Take time to read this section before you read the stories. Here are some ideas that will help you personalize the STORYTIME experience to fit your family's needs and maximize your family's enjoyment of the STORY-TIME sessions.

• Plan to use STORYTIME stories as part of a routine family activity. Bedtime, family devotions, or after-school activities are a few of the times when STORY-TIME sessions can become a part of your family's schedule.

• Follow your children's interests. Children as young as 2 will listen to and enjoy the STORYTIME stories, but if interest wanders, feel free to shorten the story or move on to other things. As often as possible, allow the children to choose the stories and activities. Let them initiate projects, and go out of your way to support these efforts at self-realization.

• Allow for plenty of repetition. Uncle Arthur's stories are easy to read over and over, and the activities are fun, but even so, you may wish for a change long before your children are ready for one. Have patience, and allow your children the opportunity to satisfy their deep interest and curiosity.

• Help your children expand their interests. Occasionally introduce new stories or activities to them. Approach these stories and activities with an attitude that shows you are anticipating adventure, and the children will soon share your sense of excitement. It won't be long before they will be enjoying a wide range of interests.

11

● Encourage your children to discuss the stories. Let them ask questions during STORYTIME sessions. The communication skills your family learns will enrich your family's relationship and their relationships with others.

● Refer to the convenient index of character traits found on page 8. You'll find this index useful when you want a story that illustrates a particular lesson.

Uncle Arthur® and the Search for Stories

Read me a story, please, Mom. Read me another one." No doubt you have heard this plea over and over. Stories appeal to the heart of every child. As they listen to stories, boys' and girls' imaginations make the scenes come alive. The children in your laps become the characters in the stories. They feel the same feelings of suspense, danger, and achievement as their story heroes and heroines.

The Uncle Arthur STORYTIME program recognizes children's love of storytelling. That's a great help to all of us parents as we teach our children valuable lessons of life. The author of the stories, Arthur Maxwell, was himself a parent of six children. In 1923 his children too begged for stories. Maxwell searched bookstores for stories that not only would entertain but also teach basic character traits such as faith, honesty, integrity, virtue, respect, and love.

Later Maxwell described this search, declaring, "There are children's storybooks in abundance on the market, but how few there are that can be read to children without some qualms of conscience." To make up for this lack of character-building material, Maxwell decided to collect and write children's stories himself.

He began with a little book he called *Uncle Arthur's Bedtime Stories.* The publisher was, at first, reluctant to publish the book. He thought children didn't care for anything but Westerns and fantasy. But to his great surprise, the public responded enthusiastically to these simple and entertaining stories of character and faith.

The demand was so great for the *Bedtime Stories* that each year Uncle Arthur was pressed to produce another volume. Forty-eight volumes were eventually published. Today, more than 42 million copies of these storybooks have been sold all over the world, translated into 22 languages.

In 1986 the producer of this work recognized the continuing need for entertaining and morally instructive children's material that would meet the highest quality standards. Uncle Arthur's stories met our requirements.

Two years of extensive research followed, conducted among parents, children, educational leaders, child development specialists, and Christian educators. We then pulled together an experienced team of designers, illustrators, and writers. The result is *Uncle Arthur's* STORYTIME Classic Edition, an effective character development program both adults and children can *enjoy* and *use*.

This Classic Edition provides a complete, entertaining, easy-to-use method for building your child's character. The rich flavor and unique heritage of Uncle Arthur's writings have been carefully preserved in these captivating stories. Charming, colorful illustrations evoke warm memories of a special time in our past.

As you continue in your STORYTIME adventures, we share with Uncle Arthur the hope that *Uncle Arthur's* STORYTIME Classic Edition will, in Uncle Arthur's words, "be a boon to teachers and parents, and a blessing to many children."

PART TWO

THE STORIES

AND THE
EXPLORING THE STORY ACTIVITIES

Bill tensed as the pitcher threw the ball, and then swung with all his might.

You know, it's not always easy to accept responsibility for what you have done, especially if it was something you knew in your heart was wrong. It can be a frightening experience. But you always feel much better after you have done the right thing, as the children in this story discovered.

Uncle Arthur

Seventeen Cowards

Bill and Susan came rushing into the house. They were in such a flurry they didn't notice Father sitting in his favorite easy chair reading a newspaper. Susan hurriedly shut the door. Both Bill and Susan flopped down on the couch, breathless and scared.

Mother, hearing the door slam, came into the room.

"Whatever is the matter, children?" she asked anxiously.

"Oh, nothing," said Bill.

"Nothing," echoed Susan.

"Yes, there is," said Father, putting down his newspaper and turning to look at them.

The children looked at him in surprise.

"I can tell something is the matter by the look on your faces. What has happened?"

"Oh, well, Dad," said Bill, wriggling uncomfortably, "you see, we were all playing ball up there on that vacant lot near old Mrs. Boliger's."

"Yes, I know where it is," said Father. "I used to play on it myself when I was a boy."

"Well, Dad, the ball . . ." Bill hesitated.

"I know what you are going to say," said Dad. "The ball went through Mrs. Boliger's window."

"Well, yes, Dad. It was an accident, but how did you know?" asked Bill.

"I just guessed," said Father. "But why are you so scared?"

"I'm not really scared, Dad," said Bill, "but Mrs. Boliger is such a mean woman. She makes such a fuss about things."

"What did you do after the window was broken?"

"We ran away," Susan said.

"You ran away!" Mother exclaimed.

"Yes," Bill said.

"How many were playing?" asked Father.

"Seventeen," said Bill.

"You mean to tell me that all 17 of you ran away, afraid of what some elderly woman might say to you?"

"Yes, Dad," said Bill, hanging his head a little.

"Well," said Father, "all I can say is that I think you were just 17 cowards, that's all."

Bill and Susan didn't like that, but they knew in their hearts that the charge was true. For a moment Bill tried to defend himself.

"But Dad, Mrs. Boliger is so cranky," he said.

"It doesn't matter how cranky she is," said Father. "If you children broke her window, you should have the courage to go and tell her you did it, and offer to pay for the damage. Why, it wouldn't have cost more than a few cents apiece. By the way, who hit the ball that broke the window?"

Bill hesitated. "Er-er-er—" he began.

"Now come on," said Father. "There couldn't have been 17 balls, nor could 17 children have smashed the window at once."

"That's right, Dad," said Bill.

"Then who hit the ball that broke the window?"

"I did," said Bill, sighing.

"I thought so," said Father, "only I wanted you to own up. And now, no matter what the others do, you both must go at once to Mrs. Boliger's, tell her you are sorry, and ask her how much the damage will cost."

"I didn't break the window," Susan cried. "I don't see why I should go."

"We couldn't," cried Bill, truly alarmed. "We simply couldn't. She is such a dreadful crank."

"But you both must," said Father sternly. "Susan, you were playing too, and are also to blame. It would be wrong to let Bill do the apologizing all by himself. The only right thing to do is to apologize. So get yourselves cleaned up, and we'll go."

"You mean you are going with us?" asked Bill.

"Yes, I am going to go with you as far as Mrs. Boliger's front gate, and then you are going to go to the door and speak to her all by yourself."

"Oh brother," Bill muttered to himself, as Susan pushed angrily passed him on the way up the stairs.

By and by the two came downstairs again, where Father was waiting for them. Mother gave an encouraging smile, as the three set out for Mrs. Boliger's.

It wasn't a very happy journey. Susan scuffed at the leaves on the walk, and glared at Bill out of the corner of her eye. Bill couldn't have been more scared if he had been on his way to prison.

"Do we really have to go?" he asked after a while.

"I'm afraid you do," said Father. "There's really no other way. And you will feel a great deal happier when you have done the right thing."

Silence fell again. They walked on, the children wishing the distance might have been 20 miles so that Father would get tired and give up.

At last they turned a corner and came to the vacant lot where the accident had taken place. Mrs. Boliger's house was in full view, and so was the broken window.

"Here we are," said Father as they reached the little white gate at the entrance to Mrs. Boliger's property. "I will wait here while you go to the house and speak to her. I'll be nearby if you need me."

There was nothing else for Bill and Susan to do now but go on alone. As the children went up the path, they felt sure that Mrs. Boliger's eyes were watching them all the way.

Bill rang the bell. It sounded loud and long, like the very knell of doom.

The door opened, and there stood Mrs. Boliger, smiling. They had not expected that.

"What can I do for you?" she said kindly.

"Well—er—well—er—," stuttered Bill, blushing.

Bill and Susan waited nervously as the door slowly opened, and there stood Mrs. Boliger.

"We—er—we were playing ball in the lot beside your house," began Susan.

"And I am the boy who—er—hit the ball that—er —broke your window this afternoon, and I am truly sorry," Bill stammered out at last. He hesitated and then turned away a little, as though he were waiting for a bomb to explode.

But it didn't. Instead he heard a very sweet voice saying, "I'm proud of you children. I have had my windows broken this way many, many times, but you are the very first who have come to tell me about it. You are a real gentleman. And you," said Mrs. Boliger, turning to Susan, "are a real young lady. You children surely must have been brought up well. You must have wonderful parents."

"Oh," said Susan, her face wreathed in a smile now that the apology was out of the way, "that's our dad over there. He happened to come along with us."

At this, Father had to come to join them.

"You have two fine children here," said Mrs. Boliger. "You know, sir, no one has ever come here before and spoken to me like this about breaking my windows."

"Well, Mrs. Boliger," said Father, "Bill, Susan, and I would like to clean up the broken glass and pay you for putting new glass in again."

"Oh, dear," said Mrs. Boliger. "I'd hate to make you pay when none of the others have. I think I have a piece of glass."

The children beamed. "Then we will put it in for you," said Father.

They talked together as they removed the broken glass and put the new glass in place. Then they said goodbye and started for home.

"I suppose," said Father, "you children aren't sorry you went to see her."

"Not one bit," said Bill.

"Why, she was really nice," Susan exclaimed.

"I never would have dreamed that Mrs. Boliger could be like that," Bill said. "I wonder why the boys say she is so mean? She isn't mean at all. She couldn't have been kinder or more considerate."

"Children say those things sometimes because they don't understand," said Father. "By the way, don't you feel better now that you have done the right thing, the brave thing that God would want you to do?"

"I sure do," Susan said.

"Boy, do I!" said Bill. "I could jump clear over the moon!"

❧ Exploring the Story ❧

You can have a successful STORYTIME™ adventure by simply reading the story to your child. The activities below are optional additions to your adventure. Use an activity after the story is read, or save it for later. The grade levels may guide your choice, but select the activity your child will most enjoy.

Discussing the Story

Why were the children in the story frightened? What happened when the children told their parents about the accident? Was it fair that Susan had to go with Bill to Mrs. Boliger's house? How would you feel if someone broke something that belonged to you?

Fun Footnotes

Baseball developed from a game milkmaids and farmhands played with an upside-down three-legged

stool during the 1300s. The batter tried to hit the ball before the ball hit the stool. The players used other stools for bases.

Stoolball was such fun that Governor Bradford, in charge of one of America's first colonies, complained that some boys even wanted to play it on Christmas Day! The game changed over the years, until in 1744 an English publication described the popular new game baseball for the first time.

STORYTIME Fun Activities

Button, Button (preschool)

You can play this game with two or more people. Use a small object, such as a button, that can be hidden easily in your hand. Ask

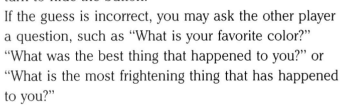

someone to guess which hand has the button. If the guess is correct, it is the other player's turn to hide the button. If the guess is incorrect, you may ask the other player a question, such as "What is your favorite color?" "What was the best thing that happened to you?" or "What is the most frightening thing that has happened to you?"

Ask questions that will help you understand how the members of your family feel inside, what makes them feel happy or sad.

Story Spots (early elementary)

Fold a clean sheet of paper in half, open it again, and sprinkle a few drops of food coloring on the paper. You can put a drop or two in the middle of the fold or scatter some drops around the page. You might want to let some of the drops run together. Fold the paper in half again and flatten it, smoothing out the drops of color. Open the paper to see the picture you have made.

Make up a story about the picture and ask someone to write it down for you, or write the story yourself. You will probably notice that as you write out your stories, you are actually writing about how you feel inside.

Round Robin Story (later elementary)

This game helps you understand how other people think. It's also a good party game, since many of these stories end up very funny! Two or any number of people can play.

Each person playing this game needs a sheet of paper and a pen or pencil. Set a timer for five minutes, and tell all the players to begin a story about anything they feel like writing about. When the time is up, have each player exchange story papers with another player and have the players continue the story written on the paper they now have. At the end of another five minutes, exchange the papers again. When it is time to end the game, announce that during the last five minutes each player should finish the story in front of him or her. Pin up the finished stories where everyone can read them or read them aloud to each other, and have a good laugh!

Hand over hand, Ronny sped to the top as the crowd watched.

STORY 2

Did you know that your real size shows when no one else in the world but you knows what is happening? I don't mean the mark on the wall that shows how tall you are; I'm talking about your inside size. Read about Ronny, and see what you think about his inside size.

Uncle Arthur

Ronny, the Rope Climber

It happened in the gym one afternoon. Mr. Skinner, the gym teacher, was talking to a group of boys near the long ropes that dangled from the ceiling.

"This is the last time this year that we are going to try to beat the school record," he said, "and I hope one of you will do it. You have sometimes come very close to it. You must each try a little bit harder."

The boys knew exactly what he meant. The school record stood at 2.1 seconds for climbing 15 feet from a standing start. Bob had done it once in 2.5 seconds, Dick in 2.4 seconds, Jerry in 2.6 seconds, and Ronny in 2.2 seconds. But no one, so far, had even equaled the record.

"Ready!" called Mr. Skinner, stopwatch in hand. "Bob first. One, two, three, go!"

Leaping as high as he could, Bob grabbed the rope

27

and shot up faster than a monkey. He touched the board at the 15-foot mark, then slid down again and waited anxiously to hear the result.

"Just under 2.4 seconds," said Mr. Skinner. "Good try, Bob, but it's not quite good enough. Let's see what Dick can do."

Dick leaped at the rope and flew up and down again in less time than it takes to tell of it. But he too was not fast enough. "Exactly 2.3 seconds," said Mr. Skinner. "Now Jerry."

Jerry tried hard too, but didn't do any better than he had before.

"Well, Ronny, it's up to you," said Mr. Skinner. "All our hopes are on you now."

By this time quite a crowd of boys had drifted into the gym. All the school had heard about the rope contest and how near a few of the best climbers were to breaking the record. Now they pressed close to see what Ronny would do this time.

Ronny wanted to beat the record more than anyone there could guess. He wasn't the best of students. He never got very good grades, but he could climb a rope. And he thought that maybe this could be one way in which he could bring honor to the school he loved so much.

"Are you ready, Ronny?" asked Mr. Skinner.

"Ready," said Ronny.

"One, two, three, go!"

With a gleam in his eye and a grim look on his face, Ronny leaped at the rope. Hand over hand, he

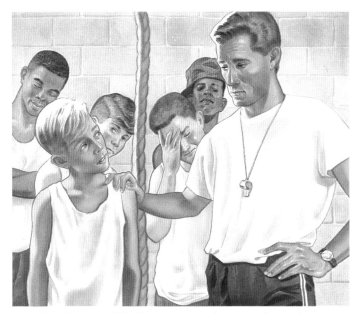

*By this time all the boys were crowding around, wondering
what had happened.*

sped to the top. A moment later he was sliding
down again.

"Two seconds!" shouted Mr. Skinner excitedly.
"Well done, my boy! Well done!"

A cheer went up all over the gym. Ronny had
beaten the record!

"But Mr. Skinner," Ronny said. "There's something
I have to tell you."

"What is it, Ronny?" asked Mr. Skinner. All the
boys leaned forward to hear what Ronny had to say.

"I'm afraid I didn't touch the marker. I missed it by
about a half inch."

Only a half inch! And nobody had seen. Not even
Mr. Skinner. It would have been so easy for Ronny to
have let everyone think he had touched the marker.
But though it meant losing the record, Ronny wouldn't
purposely mislead the others.

29

Mr. Skinner took him by the hand and looked him straight in the eye.

"I'm proud of you, Ronny," he said. "More proud than you will ever know. You have brought more glory to your school today by your honesty than you ever could by your rope climbing."

By this time all the boys were crowding around, wondering what would happen.

"Didn't he break the record?" several asked.

"No," said Mr. Skinner. "He climbed in two seconds, but he failed to touch the marker by a half inch. He is disqualified."

There were groans all over the gym. "What a shame!" cried some.

"Why didn't you keep your mouth shut, Ronny?" said others.

Mr. Skinner blew his whistle. As silence fell, he said, "Because of my inaccuracy, I am going to give Ronny one more chance."

Cheers rang out again, with shouts of "Do it this time, Ronny."

Ronny stepped to the rope.

"Take an extra-high leap," Mr. Skinner said.

Up went Ronny, faster than ever, his hand hitting the marker so everyone could see it. Down he came like a streak of lightning.

"Magnificent!" cried Mr. Skinner, clapping Ronny on the back. "You did it in 1.9 seconds and broke the record all to pieces!"

❖ Exploring the Story ❖

You can have a successful STORYTIME™ adventure by simply reading the story to your child. The activities below are optional additions to your adventure. Use an activity after the story is read, or save it for later. The grade levels may guide your choice, but select the activity your child will most enjoy.

Discussing the Story

Sometimes telling the truth is easy. If someone holds up one of your paintings and says, "Who made this beautiful picture?" it's easy to say, "I did!" What happens when someone says, "Oh, whatever happened! My favorite serving bowl—who broke this?" Is it easy to say, "I did," then? Why not?

Do you think it's important to tell the truth, even when it's hard to do? Can you think of some ways to make telling the truth easier? One good idea is to *tell the truth right away.* For instance, if you break a bowl, don't wait for your mom to ask "Who did this?" Tell her right away. It will help her feel better about the situation, especially if you apologize and explain what happened.

Fun Footnotes

Rope and the knots that make rope useful to us have a long history. One story tells of how Xerxes (pronounced **ZURK-sees**), during his invasion of Greece, marched his army across the Dardanelles (pronounced **Dar-duh-NELZ**) by way of a bridge of boats tied together with huge ropes. The ropes were made of flax and papyrus, and were 28 inches around.

STORYTIME Fun Activities

Pretzels (preschool)

Pretzels are a fun way to eat knots! They were first made by a European monk who gave them to children as a reward for learning their prayers. The bread crosses itself in the center of the pretzel as a reminder of the crossed arms of children who are praying. Try this recipe with your mom or dad, using other shapes and knots besides the traditional pretzel shape.

1 cup warm water	2 tablespoons sugar
2 packages dry yeast	3 cups flour

Dissolve the yeast in the water, add the rest of the ingredients, and knead the dough. Put the dough in an oiled bowl, cover, and let the dough rise until it has doubled its size. While the dough is rising, heat water and 2 tablespoons of baking soda in a large pot, and heat the oven to 400 degrees F. Shape pieces of dough into knots and other figures. (Take all the time you like—kids love to play with this dough.) Carefully dip each piece in the boiling water for 5-10 seconds, and place on a greased cookie sheet. Brush with beaten egg, sprinkle with salt, and bake for 12-15 minutes.

Rope Wrap (early elementary)

You can use rope to put a new face on a tired lamp base, or a metal or plastic container you want to make into a planter, or turn a tin can into a pencil holder. Use rough hemp if you want a natural look; colored cord or yarn if you like bright or delicate colors.

Apply glue or epoxy a little at a time. Begin at the bottom, and wrap the rope around and around the container. For a more complicated pattern, you might want to try braiding the rope before you wrap it.

You can decorate the rope as you go by stringing beads directly on the rope, or tying cord onto your main rope as a fringe. You can tie beads or other decorations in the fringe.

Teakettle (later elementary)

"Knot" and "not" are examples of homonyms, words that sound the same but are spelled differently. Think up a sentence using a set of homonyms, and repeat it to the rest of the family, except substitute the word "teakettle" for the homonyms. Here is an example. Can you figure out the homonyms that belong in this sentence?

Please put "teakettle" shoes over "teakettle."

ANSWERS
(unscramble words for answers)
ihret, hetre

PAIR   PEAR

A blast of heat hit Kim's face as she opened the oven door. Was it too hot or not hot enough?

It's good to want to be independent and learn to do things on your own. It's another thing altogether to want to do things your own way, without first making sure that you really know what to do. That kind of attitude leads to trouble, as Kim sadly discovered.

Uncle Arthur

Kim's Cake

I wish you would let me make a cake all by myself one day," said Kim.

"Someday," said Mother, "when you are older."

"But why can't I do it now?"

"Because there are so many things that might go wrong, and we can't afford to risk spoiling all the things that go into it."

"But I know I can do it all by myself," insisted Kim. "Couldn't I make a cake for my birthday party?"

"You may make one, dear," said Mother, "but not all by yourself. I must be with you and see that you do everything right."

"But that's just what I don't want you to do," said Kim. "I don't like people telling me what to do."

"Maybe not," said Mother, "but there is such a

thing as being too independent. That's when things go wrong."

"Then I can't make my own cake all by myself?"

"Not this time, dear."

This should have settled the matter, but not with Kim. She kept on pleading and teasing until at last Mother said, "Very well, Kim. If you must make your own cake, make it, and I'll keep out of the way. You can do it all by yourself, but don't blame me if something goes wrong. Just remember, though, that good or bad, you and your friends will have to eat it at the party. I won't make another one."

Kim was delighted. Now her dream was to come true. She would make a cake all by herself. Quickly she put on her apron, found the cookbook, and turned to the recipe that she liked the best. Carefully she measured the flour, the butter, the sugar, the raisins, just as she had seen Mother do so often. One by one she put them into a bowl and began to mix them.

Kim remembered that Mother had said that everything should be mixed very thoroughly. So she mixed and mixed, using the right number of eggs and milk.

Next Kim found the right size cake pans, greased them well, and lined them with paper, just as Mother always did. She poured the mixture into the cake pans with the aid of a big wooden spoon. So far, so good. Now for the baking.

She had turned on the oven when she started to prepare the cake, and it was now quite hot. But was it too hot or not hot enough? That worried her. She knew that it was most important that the heat should be just right, but how could she tell what it should be? Oh dear, she hadn't thought about that. Perhaps she had better ask Mother, just so there would be no mistake.

"Mother! How hot should the oven be when I put the cake in?"

There was no answer. Mother had gone out! Kim had to decide for herself.

In went the cake. But Kim was troubled by the blast of heat that hit her face as she opened the door. Surely it was too hot. Wasn't it? How terrible not to know! Perhaps, after all that she had done right so far, the cake would be burned.

Kim couldn't rest. What was happening in the oven? She opened the door and looked in, pulling the cake toward her so she could see it better. It was starting to rise and seemed to be all right. She was so pleased that she closed the door with a bang.

A little later she began to worry again. Was the cake baking properly?

She looked inside again. There it was, browning nicely, but just about the size it had been before. It hadn't risen any more. Not even a little bit.

Kim closed the door again. She was really worried now. What could be the matter? She knew enough about making cakes to know that if it didn't rise properly at first it wouldn't rise later and then, oh dear, it would come out hard as a rock.

She waited and waited, watching the clock to be sure to give the cake just the right time that the cookbook said. She opened the oven door again, but the cake was just the same size, only a little browner. How she wished Mother would come back! Maybe she would suggest something to do before it was too late. But she didn't come.

Somehow Mother knew exactly how long it takes to bake a cake. She stayed away until it was just time to take it out of the oven. Then the kitchen door opened and in she came.

"How's the cake, Kim?" she asked.

Kim said nothing. At that very moment she was lifting the cake out of the oven, hoping that Mother wouldn't see it. Something had gone wrong, but what that something was she couldn't tell.

"Rather flat, isn't it, dear?" said Mother.

Still Kim said nothing, but there were tears in her eyes now.

"What did I do wrong?" she said at last.

"I'm not sure I know," said Mother. "I wasn't here to see. But I can make a pretty good guess."

"What is it then?"

"It seems to have been mixed all right, but it didn't rise properly. Did you move it while it was rising? Or maybe you banged the oven door."

Kim remembered all too well. "I suppose I did," she said, feeling very sorry now.

"Well anyway, at least you have a cake for the party," said Mother.

There was nothing else Kim could do. It was either this cake at the party or no cake at all.

"Oh, no, no!" cried Kim. "We can't have this. You'll have to make another one."

"Impossible," said Mother. "You wanted to make it all by yourself, and I let you on condition that you must use it at the party, good or bad. Of course you must stand by the bargain."

There was nothing else to do. It was either this cake or no cake at all.

So when her friends came to the party, Kim brought her cake to the table. They nearly had to send for an ax to cut it. It was just that hard. Of course the other little girls had a lot of fun over it. Kim tried to be brave, and said that it was all her fault. But to herself she said she never would try to do things "all by herself" again, when Mother advised her not to.

❖ Exploring the Story ❖

You can have a successful STORYTIME™ adventure by simply reading the story to your child. The activities below are optional additions to your adventure. Use an activity after the story is read, or save it for later. The grade levels may guide your choice, but select the activity your child will most enjoy.

Discussing the Story

What do you think Kim's problem was in this story? Was it just that she wanted to make the cake herself? Discuss some other reasons. What's good about wanting to learn how to do things yourself?

Do you remember what Kim's mother said when Kim wanted to know if she could bake the cake all by herself? She wanted Kim to wait until she was a little older. Kim had learned a lot about making cakes, but not quite enough to do it herself. Do you have some ideas about what Kim should have done, instead of demanding her own way? Add more ideas to the list below.

1. Trusted her mother to know what was best.
2. Waited patiently for the proper time.

Fun Footnotes

There are many interesting chemical reactions that happen in a cake as it bakes. Baking soda, which makes cakes rise, reacts with acid to make the tiny bubbles of carbon dioxide. The bubbles get bigger as the batter gets warmer. The milk and egg proteins in the batter change shape and get firm around the bubbles. Flour also strengthens the walls around the gas

40

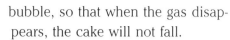

bubble, so that when the gas disappears, the cake will not fall.

If you bump the cake before the batter is set around the gas bubbles, you will cause the cake to fall. It will also fall if you let in cold air from an open oven door, causing the gas in the cake to contract.

STORYTIME Fun Activities

Peanut Butter Balls (preschool)

You can make cookies without measuring or baking. You will need a mixing pan, a big spoon, peanut butter, honey or dark corn syrup, and milk powder. You can also add raisins, coconut, and chocolate chips, if you like.

Put a big spoonful of peanut butter in your pan, and pour in a little honey or syrup. Mix in raisins or other ingredients now, if you are going to use them. Mix in milk powder a little at a time, until you have a stiff dough. Roll pieces of the dough into balls, and share them with your friends!

Can You Follow Directions? (early elementary)

Use a stopwatch or other timer to see how quickly you can follow these instructions. (You can add most of your own instructions, and use this as a party game, if you like. To be fair, don't include anyone who has played the game before.)

1. Write your name at the top of a sheet of paper.
2. Read all of the instructions before doing anything else.
3. Circle all the vowels in your name.
4. Count the letters in your name and write the number in the lower right-hand corner of the page.
5. Add 2 to your first number, and write your sum in the lower left-hand corner of the page.
6. Add the numbers in the two bottom corners, and write this sum in the middle of the page.
7. Draw a rectangle around the largest number you have written down.
8. Divide the rectangle into four approximately equal parts.
9. Fill in one fourth of the rectangle.
10. Now that you have read these instructions, do not go back to complete the instructions for 3 through 10.
11. Stop the stopwatch.

Pyramid (later elementary)

Can you follow these instructions without anyone helping you? You can decorate the pyramid that you make, and put several together to make curious shapes.

1. Make a triangle with equal sides on a colored piece of paper. Start with a line 10 inches long. Put a

ruler at one end of the line, and make a curve 10 inches away from this point. Put the ruler at the other end of the line, and make another curve 10 inches away. Mark the point where your two curves cross, and use this for the third point of your triangle.

2. Fold each point of the triangle to its opposite edge. Fold the paper in half again. Open up the triangle. Fold the other two points of the triangle in the same way, to make the pattern shown by the dotted lines.

3. Number the folded sections as in the illustration, and cut away the unnumbered parts.

4. Fold side 1 over side 5 and glue. Now fold sides 2, 6, and 7 under, and glue.

"I was only 5 when we started," said Grandma. "It was a journey of 3,000 miles across mountains and prairies with no roads."

Are you lucky enough to have a grandma? If so, the first chance you get, ask her to tell you some of the things that happened to her when she was a little girl. I wouldn't be surprised if they prove to be the most interesting stories you've ever heard.

Uncle Arthur

The Mysterious Rider

Grandma McAlpine was nearly 80 years of age, but she could remember almost everything about her childhood. How her grandchildren did love to listen to her!

One evening Frank and Bessie were visiting Grandma in her home. Soon they were trying to persuade her to tell them one of her grand old stories of the long ago.

"Please, Grandma!" urged Bessie. "Just one. We love to listen to your stories."

"Yes, please!" chimed in Frank. "You know, Grandma, that one you promised to tell us, about the mysterious rider."

A smile came over Grandma's face.

"All right then," said Grandma. "Make yourselves comfortable, and I'll tell you now."

Frank and Bessie seated themselves as close to

Grandma as possible, and looked up expectantly into her face.

"It happened nearly 75 years ago this October," Grandma began. "I was a little girl of 5, but I remember it all as clearly as if it had happened yesterday.

"The real beginning of my story, however, came a hundred years or so before that. My great-grandfather 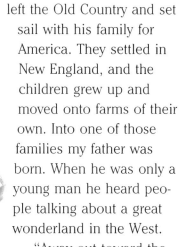 left the Old Country and set sail with his family for America. They settled in New England, and the children grew up and moved onto farms of their own. Into one of those families my father was born. When he was only a young man he heard people talking about a great wonderland in the West.

"Away out toward the sunset, it was said, there were thousands and thousands of square miles of marvelous forests where grew the greatest trees anyone had ever seen. The soil was so rich that it would grow finer wheat than any farmer had ever raised. Everything was there that could be desired.

"My father listened. It seemed promising to him. It was just what he wanted. He talked to my mother, and finally they decided to go.

"There were no trains then, and no roads. It meant a journey of 3,000 miles across open prairies, through forests and rivers and over high mountains. They had to crowd all their goods into one old covered wagon, drawn by two oxen."

"Tell us about the covered wagon," said Bessie.

"Well, just a word," said Grandma, "for we haven't got to the real story yet. Most of the covered wagons were built of strong, thick planks. They were made long and narrow, so that they could be used as boats in crossing rivers."

"Did you travel in one of those covered wagons?" asked Bessie, her eyes wide open with wonder.

"Yes, I surely did," said Grandma. "I was only 5 when we started out, but I can still see everything that happened on that long, long journey."

"How long did it take?" asked Frank.

"More than six months," said Grandma. "We left our home in April, as soon as the snow was gone. It was October before we caught sight of Mount Hood in Oregon, far, far in the West. Seven or eight other wagons were in our caravan, and day by day we moved slowly on, just as fast as the oxen could take us.

"Some days it was very, very hot, and then we would all get terribly thirsty. I think the oxen felt it more than we did, because they had most of the work to do. I remember one day we had traveled many miles without water. Suddenly the oxen stopped. They refused to haul the wagon another yard. Father took the yokes off them, and suddenly they started to run. They had either seen or smelled water more than a mile away, but they were too weary to take the wagon with them."

"Did you catch them?" asked Frank.

"Oh, yes," said Grandma. "That was easy. They only wanted to drink. Then we started off again."

"But the rider—the mysterious rider—when did he appear?" asked Bessie.

"Just you wait a minute," said Grandma. "We're coming to that all in good time. Some other things

"We were all alone on the mountain summit with only enough food to last two or three days."

were to happen first. We rode on day after day, week after week, month after month. The poor oxen became more and more footsore and weary. Father did not dare to let them rest very much, for he knew that he had to get over the mountains before the snow began falling.

"The food began to give out. We were allowed just so much a day and no more, for Father said that if we were delayed and ran out of food, we would die on the way.

"The oxen became more and more tired, and Father grew more and more worried, as we moved on westward. At long last we started to climb the Cascade Mountains. I can't think how anyone ever found a way across, for there were no beautiful roads as there are today. It was all so wild and rocky that we were nearly jolted out of the wagon many times. Still we went on, climbing up and up, with the oxen panting and sweating in front, and Father shoving his hardest behind.

"At last we reached the summit. In the distance we could see Mount Hood, its white peak gleaming in the morning sun. We knew that there would still be many more days of travel, but it seemed to us that the journey was almost over.

"That very morning, something dreadful happened. One of our oxen died. The climb up the mountains had been too much for it. We were left with only one ox, and one could never pull that heavy wagon. Father was at his wits' end to know what to do. He talked to the people in the other wagons. They were sorry, but they could not do anything. Their oxen, too, were almost worn out, and their food was almost gone. They felt that they had to go on without us, and so they did.

"I shall never forget how we all felt when the last wagon had gone out of sight down the steep, rough trail. We were alone on the summit of the Cascade Mountains with no means of getting away, and with only enough food to last us two or three days.

"Night came on. It was very cold. Father wondered whether the snow would come, and what we would do then. He kindled a fire, Mother gave us something to eat, and I was put to bed. Father and Mother sat up and talked of what they could do.

"By and by Father said to Mother, 'Surely the great God who has brought us in safety all this long way through so many troubles will not desert us now. Let us kneel here on the mountaintop and tell Him of our plight.'

"They knelt in the dark with the cold wind blowing around them, and told God all that had happened. They told Him how they trusted Him to take care of them. Then they arose, and soon after that they tried to sleep.

"The night wore on. The bright, cold stars looked down upon our little lonely camp. Dawn was just beginning to break when suddenly Father sat up. The silence had been broken by strange sounds.

"Clippety-clop, clippety-clop, clippety-clop.

" 'Horses!' whispered Father.

" 'Do you think it's Indians?' whispered Mother, sitting up beside him.

" 'I don't know,' said Father. 'We must wait and see.'

"They stood quietly beside the wagon, listening and watching as the sound of the horses' hooves came ever nearer and nearer.

The silence was broken by strange sounds. In the dim light, Father could just make out the form of a man on horseback.

"Suddenly out of the darkness came a voice. 'Hi there!' cried someone.

" 'Who is it?' called Father.

" 'A friend' was the answer.

"In the dim morning light Father could just make out the form of a man on horseback, with another horse beside him. He walked over toward the stranger.

" 'Are you in trouble?' asked the mysterious rider.

" 'We are,' said Father. 'Desperate trouble. One of our oxen has died, and we are stranded here with hardly any food left.'

"The mysterious rider took us to his own home and fed us. Then he lent us another ox, so that we were able to reach the end of our journey in safety."

"What was the name of the mysterious rider?" asked Frank.

"He never told us," said Grandma. "He just said we were to call him the Colonel, which we have done ever since."

"But how did he happen to find you?" asked Bessie.

"Ah," said Grandma, "that is the most wonderful part of the story, for there was no telephone in those days and no telegraph. All Father could do was to tell God and trust Him to do all the rest.

"All my life," she added, "I have never forgotten that terrible night on the mountain, and the mysterious rider who came to our rescue. Children, I want you always to remember that the great God whom we love and serve never forgets His own."

51

❖ Exploring the Story ❖

You can have a successful STORYTIME™ adventure by simply reading the story to your child. The activities below are optional additions to your adventure. Use an activity after the story is read, or save it for later. The grade levels may guide your choice, but select the activity your child will most enjoy.

Discussing the Story

There are many questions that we don't know the answers to. For example, we don't understand how birds know how to build nests. What are some other examples? We often don't know how God manages to take care of us. We have faith in God when we believe something about Him that we don't completely understand. What are some other things that you believe about God, though you don't know how He does it?

Fun Footnotes

The covered wagons that America's westward traveling settlers used were often called "prairie schooners." Schooners were ships with several masts and sails. *Their* name came from a New England word, *scoon,* which meant "glide," or "slide," as when a flat stone skips along the surface of the water. Not only did the billowing canvas covers of the covered wagons look like sails skimming over the oceanlike prairies, but the wagon bodies were shaped like boats, too. They were longer at the top than at the bottom.

The wagon bodies were only 3½ feet wide and 10 feet long. Measure out a space that size in your living room, and see if you could move all your belongings in a wagon that small!

STORYTIME Fun Activities

Camp Biscuits (preschool)

It took a long time for the settlers traveling west to reach their new homes. They had to carry food that would last a long time without a refrigerator. Beans and flour lasted as long as they were dry.

You can make biscuits that are fun to cook over a campfire. Just follow the recipe below.

2 cups flour
3 teaspoons baking
powder
¾ teaspoon salt
¾ cup milk

Mix these ingredients, and knead lightly. Add a little milk if necessary, for a slightly sticky dough. Make a rope of dough about the size of your thumb, and wrap it several times around a stick. A fork in the stick helps the dough stay on, but you can use a straight stick, too. Hold the stick over hot coals, and

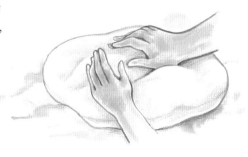

watch the bread swell and brown. You might want to find a way to prop the stick up, because biscuits take 8-10 minutes to bake. Remember to turn it several times so the bread can bake on all sides.

The Circuit Ridin' Preacher (early elementary)

Western settlements were small and were separated by long distances. There weren't enough preachers to go around. Often the settlers had to wait months before a preacher came for a visit, and they were glad to see him. They would have church services whatever day of the week he was there, and he would hold funeral services and wedding services for those who had died or had gotten married since he had visited last.

The following song about the circuit ridin' preacher is sung to a tune you probably already know. You might remember the tune as "John Brown's Body," or "The Battle Hymn of the Republic," which were Civil War rallying songs. The chorus uses a different tune, "Leaning on the Everlasting Arms." This is a fun song to sing.

> The circuit ridin' preacher used to ride across
>   the land,
> With a rifle on his saddle and a Bible in his hand.
> He told the prairie people all about the
>   Promised Land
> As he went ridin' (singin') down the trail.
> Chorus:
> Leaning, leaning, safe and secure from all alarm;
> Leaning, leaning, leaning on the everlasting arms.
>
> —Tim Spencer

Wagon Wheels (later elementary)

You can use macaroni products to make fun miniatures of prairie schooners and log houses. Design a shoe-box panorama of a wagon going up a mountain pass, or a circle of wagons around a campfire in the prairie, or a homecoming. You can also use the figures to decorate place cards for a Western party.

Make the prairie schooners out of wheel macaroni, cardboard, and corn husks. Cut out the wagon bodies first, using the pattern below. Paint these black, if you like. Paint the macaroni wheels red or brown, and glue four onto each wagon body. Cut out the corn husks, and soak them till they are soft. Drape them over a pencil, propping them in the right shape for canvas covers, until they dry. You can also use white material soaked in a sugar solution instead of corn husks. Cut a front and back for the wagon covers, if you want even more realistic results, and glue the covers to the wagon bodies.

Make log cabins and sheds by gluing spaghetti pieces to construction paper already cut the proper size for walls and roofs. Glue the walls together, and paint.

*Richard was clapping his hands in excitement when the wind
shifted and tragedy struck.*

If you have ever tried to invent something like the boy in this story tried to do, you probably remember all the work that went into your project. And despite all your work, your project probably didn't turn out quite the way you hoped—not the first time, anyway. One of the first rules an inventor (or explorer, or artist, or anyone else who wants to make a success of his or her ventures) learns is "Try, try, again."

Uncle Arthur

Richard's Rubbish Heap

Richard was as excited as a dog with 10 tails. He had always wanted to "invent" something, and now he had done so. His big "air balloon" was almost ready. He had been working on it for several weeks. There were just a few more odds and ends to fix. Then Richard would be able to set light to the cotton wool at the bottom and watch the big paper bag fill with hot air and soar away into the sky.

It was going to be a big day for Richard. All his friends were coming to see the great sight. Richard had told them all about it long before he had even worked out the design. Now he was sure their eyes would pop out when they saw the balloon completed.

It was something to see, too, I can tell you. Six feet high and four feet in diameter, it had been no small job to build. Richard had first made a framework of very light, strong wire. Then he had cut long strips of tissue paper of various colors into the proper shape, like slices of an orange peel. When the strips were pasted together, they made a big paper globe around the wire frame. What a task pasting the edges of that paper had been, and how many times it had torn or got stuck in the wrong place!

At the very bottom of the frame was a circle of wire. In the center of the circle of wire, supported on two cross wires, was a pad of cotton wool. This cotton wool was to be set alight, at the right moment, to heat the air inside the balloon. At last all the preparations were made. All Richard's friends were standing around waiting impatiently for the moment when the balloon would sail aloft.

Richard, however, was not in a hurry. He wanted to enjoy this moment of triumph. He had worked so hard, and had looked forward to this moment for so long. He kept explaining how he had designed the balloon. He told why he was sure it would rise into the air. He answered, over and over again, all the questions his friends asked about it.

At last, he applied a match to the cotton wool. It flared up, and all the children stood back to watch. The air inside became hotter and hotter, and the big tissue-paper bag gradually filled out.

"It's lifting!" cried Richard excitedly. "It's lifting! It's going up!"

He was clapping his hands in excitement when suddenly a puff of wind blew the flame toward the tissue paper. There was no time to save it. In a moment, the whole balloon became a mass of flames and dropped to the ground.

Poor Richard! He was heartbroken. He ran indoors, anxious to get away from all his friends. They had expected so much of him and his much advertised "invention." He felt ashamed that he had said so much about it before it had been proved a success. So much work had gone into that balloon, too. It had taken all his spare time for weeks! Now there was nothing left but a heap of ashes and tangled wire.

Father found Richard in his bedroom, weeping his heart out. "Don't worry too much about it," said Father. "Much worse things happen in this old world. What really matters is not that the balloon is all burned up, but that you worked so hard trying to make something worthwhile."

"But it's all wasted," wailed Richard.

"No, it is not wasted," said Father. "Think of all you have learned. Think of all that you have read about balloons, and all the little tricks that you've discovered about bending wire and sticking tissue paper together. All that isn't lost. It will prove useful someday; wait and see."

"But I really did want to invent something," sobbed Richard.

"I know," said Father, "but worthwhile things don't get invented as quickly as that. Think of Edison and how long he experimented before he invented the electric light. The same is true for his phonograph and all the

59

*"Find out what was wrong and make it right. That's how all
worthwhile inventions come about," said Father.*

other priceless things he gave the world. Do you think
he discovered them all at once? No indeed. He
worked and worked over them, trying and failing and
trying again."

"For weeks and weeks, as I did?" asked Richard.

"For years and years," comforted Father. "And he
had so many failures that it is a wonder he carried on
as he did. You should just see his rubbish heap."

"His rubbish heap?" questioned Richard in
surprise.

"Yes indeed," said Father. "To this day it is shown
to all who visit his old workshop. It is just outside the
window by his bench. Every time an experiment went
wrong, Edison would throw it out the window and
start again. He didn't let failure discourage him, and
neither must you. Build another balloon and a better

one next time. Invent one that won't catch fire. Find out what was wrong and make it right. That's how all worthwhile inventions come about."

"I suppose that if Edison had a rubbish heap, I shouldn't worry too much about my little pile of ashes," said Richard, smiling at last.

"That's right," agreed Father. "That's the spirit that wins. Every real inventor has a rubbish heap. You've made a good start toward success already."

❖ Exploring the Story ❖

You can have a successful STORYTIME™ adventure by simply reading the story to your child. The activities below are optional additions to your adventure. Use an activity after the story is read, or save it for later. The grade levels may guide your choice, but select the activity your child will most enjoy.

Discussing the Story

Most of the great things accomplished in this world have taken a good deal of effort. Scientists struggle with many different solutions before they discover the right one. Writers may write for many years before they get published or win an award for their writing. Painters paint many paintings before they win recognition. In the process of trying things over and over until you find the very best way, you learn a lot, you change, you grow and become a better person.

Is there anything you have been trying to do? Do you have a dream of doing something great? Don't depend on luck. Look ahead. What do you think you'll need to do to make your dream come true? Find out and then try again and again!

Fun Footnotes

Thomas Edison was responsible for about 1,300 inventions. In a guestbook that had an "Interested In" column, Edison wrote "Everything." He didn't often have an easy time coming up with his inventions, however. In his search for a new storage battery, he failed with 10,000 experiments before he found what he wanted. When someone commented on the large number of failures before he achieved results, Edison said, "Results? Why, I have gotten a lot of results. I know 10,000 things that won't work."

STORYTIME Fun Activities

Mary's Lamb (preschool)

Can you guess what Edison's favorite invention has to do with Mary's little lamb? The record player was Edison's favorite invention, and the first words he recorded were "Mary had a little lamb!"

Edison's first record was a small metal cylinder wrapped in tinfoil. When Edison said "Mary had a little lamb" into the mouthpiece, the cylinder turned, and a needle scratched dents in the tinfoil. In order to play the record, another needle followed the dents.

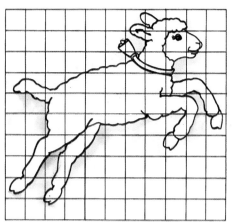

Bumping into the dents made the needle shake and vibrate. When the sound from the vibrating needle was made a little louder, you could hear "Mary had a little lamb."

Here's an activity for you to try. Put a piece of aluminum foil on a soft surface such as a thick, slightly spongy, vinyl place mat. Tape a paper cutout of a lamb (one you have drawn or found in a coloring book) on the foil, and punch holes all around the cutout. Take off the paper cutout, and tape the foil to a lampshade. Watch the lamb shine through!

Helix (early elementary)

You can use a hanging helix to show that heat rises, the principle Richard depended upon to make his balloon rise. Cut a paper plate in a spiral so it looks like a snake. Punch a tiny hole in the center of the plate so you can push a thread through and knot it.

You may want to tie the thread to a pencil to use as a holder.

Turn on an electric stove burner as hot as it will go (with your parents' help, of course). Hang the helix above the burner just far enough so it won't scorch. The rising heat waves will make your helix spin. Hold your helix away from the burner, and watch the helix slow and stop. Try hanging the helix over other heat sources, such as a radiator or wood stove.

Movie Flip Book (later elementary)

Edison invented one of the first working motion picture machines. Motion pictures are really many still pictures that are shown so fast (about 24 pictures a second) that we see one smoothly running picture.

You can use this same idea to make your own short "movie." Use the corner of a small notebook. Start at the back of the notebook, because these will be the first pages that flip past your thumb. Draw a simple picture that shows the beginning of some movement such as a stone ready to roll down a hill, or a batter beginning to swing at a ball. On each of the following pages, draw the stone a little bit further down the hill, or the bat a little closer to the ball.

The more pictures you have, the longer your "movie" will be. Try to make 20 or more pictures.

*With great care Elsie wrote the letter, underlining all the
things they wanted most.*

If you want to have the happiest Christmas ever, try this little trick. Plan to make someone else happy. I think you will find, like Nellie, that no gift you receive will make you happier than watching someone else's joy on Christmas!

Uncle Arthur

Nellie's Wish

School was over. Vacation time had begun. Everyone was looking forward to Christmas Day. How slowly the days seemed to pass! It seemed as if Christmas would never come. Outdoors it was too cold to play, and indoors there seemed nothing to do without forever getting in Mother's way.

"Oh, what can we do?" said Nellie to her sister Elsie.

"Let's write that letter to Santa Claus we were going to send him."

"If you want to," said Nellie. "But do you know, I believe Santa Claus is Daddy dressed up."

"Do you?"

"Yes. Last Christmas I kept one eye open till some-one came into my room to fill my stocking, and I'm sure it was Daddy in his bathrobe."

67

"But let's write the letter anyway," urged little Elsie.

"Oh, yes; that will be fun, won't it? What shall we ask him to send us?"

"Let's get some paper and a pencil first, so we won't forget anything."

"I'll run and get some," said Nellie, and off she went, coming back in a few minutes with enough paper for a long letter.

Since Elsie had just learned to write, they agreed that she should write the letter. Nellie would sit by to tell her how to spell the words.

"Before you begin, let's try to think of what we would like most," said Nellie.

They talked the matter over very seriously, and decided that they wanted a large number of things. Elsie was sure she needed a box of paints, a baby doll, a doll buggy, a ball, lots of candy, oranges, and apples, and a music box.

Nellie had bigger ideas. She wanted a scooter, some good books with pictures in them, a big box of chocolates, and, above all things, a doll that could talk and move its eyes. "I really don't think he will be able to carry them all," said Nellie.

"Oh, I do," said Elsie. "He has a big bag."

"Yes, and there is no harm in putting them all down."

So they did. With much care little Elsie wrote the letter, underlining all the things they wanted most. At last the letter was finished and ready to be placed in an envelope. Nellie read it over, all the way from "Dear Santa Claus" down to "Hoping to see you soon." Then she gave a little sigh, and put it on the table.

"Why, what's the matter?" asked Elsie.

Nellie was silent a moment. Then she said, "I think it is a rather selfish letter."

"Why?"

"Because we have asked only for things for ourselves. There's not one thing for anyone else."

"That's right. What should we do? Do we have to write it all over again?"

"Oh, no; that would take too long. Why not add a postscript?"

"What's that?"

"Just a few words at the bottom."

"All right. What shall we say?"

"I would like to see some of the poor children at school get some nice things like those we have asked Santa Claus to send us."

"So would I."

"There's Kitty Gordon," said Nellie. "She's such a nice girl. But her mother is so poor that I don't suppose she will get many Christmas presents at all."

"Won't she really?"

"I don't suppose so."

"Then let's ask for something nice for her. I'm sure she'd like a pretty doll too."

"Yes," said Nellie, "put that down. Then the letter will be all right, I think."

So Elsie carefully added the words "Please see that Kitty Gordon gets a beautiful doll." Then they folded the letter, put it in the envelope, and stuck an old stamp on it. Finally they handed it to Mother, and asked her to see that it was mailed.

Christmas morning came, and with it all the glorious fun of emptying stockings and examining the presents that were piled under the tree. Nellie and Elsie were as happy as children could be. They shrieked with delight as they opened each package and found something for which they had asked in their letter. Of course, they did not get all their requests, but they got enough to make them feel sure Santa had read their message.

But one thing was wrong, at least so far as Nellie was concerned. She did not say anything about it till she had opened all her packages. Then she began to look just a little bit worried. She turned all the tissue paper over again and again and looked under the bed, even in the closet, but in vain. The thing she wanted most of all was not there.

"What's the matter, Nellie?" asked Elsie. "Haven't you got enough things?"

"Oh, Elsie," said Nellie, "I know I have some lovely things, but it isn't here."

"What do you mean?"

"Oh, I did so want a baby doll that says 'Mama.' "

"Maybe he took one to Kitty Gordon instead of you."

"Maybe so," sighed Nellie. "But I didn't really mean for him to do that."

Hardly had she said it when she realized how really mean it was. She had all these beautiful things,

Nellie was walking back to her seat when suddenly she pointed to the window and cried, "Look! Look!"

and she wondered whether Kitty had anything nearly as nice. All day she felt unhappy about it, and as she played with her new toys, she kept thinking, *Should I have taken Kitty some of my things?*

In the evening Nellie and Elsie went to a party that was being given by the woman next door. There were several other little girls there, and they had a fine time together. After refreshments—and what good food it was!—they all went into another room. There was a beautiful Christmas tree covered with pretty shiny decorations and little colored lights. It was a very thrilling sight.

But the thing that took Nellie's attention most was a beautiful doll that was lying among all the other gifts placed beneath the tree. Her heart beat fast as she thought that perhaps now her great wish was to be granted. They played all kinds of games around the

71

tree. Then at last the presents were distributed. Only one question was in Nellie's mind: who was going to get the doll?

Impatiently she waited and waited while every other child received a gift. Now there was just one present left beside the tree. It was the doll.

"This," said the woman, "is for—"

"Nellie," said all the children, for they saw that she had nothing from the tree so far.

Nellie blushed and jumped up from her seat. Taking the doll from the woman, she hugged it tightly to herself.

Nellie was walking back to her seat when suddenly she pointed to the window and cried, "Oh, look! look!"

Everybody looked, but there was nothing to be seen. The shades were up, but outside all was dark and still.

"What was it?" cried all the children.

"It was Kitty Gordon. She was looking in the window, and I'm sure she was crying. Oh, I must go find her!"

Without another word Nellie rushed to the front door and ran out, not even waiting to put on her coat. Far down the street under a light Nellie thought she saw a little figure.

"Kitty!" she cried. "Kitty! Come here."

But Kitty went on, and Nellie had to run the whole length of the block before she caught up with her friend.

"Oh, Kitty!" she panted. "I've brought you something. Please stop and take it."

Kitty stood there in the street looking in amazement at the wonderful thing she held in her arms. It was a doll that could shut its eyes and say "Mama."

"For me?" she said.

"Yes, yes, for you," said Nellie. "I want you to have it most of all." Then she turned and ran back to the house, feeling happier than she had ever felt before.

That night before she went to sleep, she remembered the note she had added to her letter to Santa Claus. Nellie was thankful she had helped to answer it.

❖ Exploring the Story ❖

You can have a successful STORYTIME™ adventure by simply reading the story to your child. The activities below are optional additions to your adventure. Use an activity after the story is read, or save it for later. The grade levels may guide your choice, but select the activity your child will most enjoy.

Discussing the Story

What do you think is most important about Christmas? Make two lists. In the first list, write down the most important *things* in Christmas, such as a Christmas tree, or a manger scene. In the second list, write down the most important *experiences* at Christmas time, such as feeling close to your family, or opening presents.

Fun Footnotes

Evergreens have decorated homes and public buildings since ancient times. As Christmas developed into a holiday, families brought evergreens into their homes and churches to make them festive. An old English rhyme says, "Holly and ivy, box and bay, put in the church on Christmas Day."

Tradition sets Martin Luther as the first person to decorate the Christmas tree with lights. The lights were to represent the lovely stars shining above Bethlehem.

STORYTIME Fun Activities

3-D Paper Ornaments (preschool)

Paper ornaments can decorate your windows, presents, or tree, and they are quick and easy to make. Find or draw a symmetrical design (meaning both halves the same) such as a bell. For each bell ornament, you will need to cut four or five bells the same size out of colored paper. Decorate one side of each paper bell and fold each one in half, decorated side in. Glue the undecorated sides together, as shown in the illustration.

If you want to add a real jingle bell to the bottom of your paper bell for a "clapper," don't include a paper clapper in your original design. Loop the jingle bell through a piece of string or gold cord. Glue the two lengths of string or cord inside the paper bell just before you glue the two paper halves together, leaving enough cord at the top of the bell to tie into a loop, so you can hang the ornament.

Potato Print Christmas Cards (early elementary)

You can make your own Christmas cards by decorating heavy paper with potato prints. Decide on a simple design such as a pine tree, a star, or a bell. With Mom's or Dad's help, cut a slice off a large potato so that the flat space left on the potato is big enough for your design. Place your design on the flat space of the potato. Cut into the potato, following the outline of your design, being careful not to cut inside your design. Cut away the potato on the outside of the design. The design should rise at least a half inch above the rest of the potato, which serves as a handle.

Dip the potato printer in poster paint, just coating the printing surface, and print a row of trees, stars, bells, or whatever your design, across your paper. You can use an old toothbrush, comb, and a contrasting color of paint to make splatters across this design. Or add glitter for a festive look.

Bag It (later elementary)

Do you need a gift idea that will work for just about everybody on your Christmas list? Make some shoe bags. Shoe bags are good for anyone who travels and hates to pack dirty shoes with his or her clothes, but they are useful in many other ways, too. Fill them with nuts in the shell, candy, ribbon and lace scraps for making doll clothes, or small scraps of wood for your little brother to stack and glue.

To make two shoe bags large enough for your dad's shoes, you will need four pieces of material each 10 inches by 18 inches. You can make smaller bags for other purposes. If you want to decorate the bags, decorate the pieces of material before you sew them into bags.

For each bag, put two pieces of material right sides together. Sew around three edges, leaving one and a half inches on the top side to hem under. Fold the top edge down a quarter inch to the inside of the bag, and sew. Fold it down another inch, to make a packet for a string or ribbon you will use as a draw-string, and sew. Use a safety pin to thread the string or ribbon through the packet. The bags make a nice gift by themselves, or you can fill 'em up!

Mike worked the big bellows that made the fire white-hot, while his father hammered the heated iron.

There is a proverb that says "One who does his work well will not stand before ordinary men; he will stand before kings." If you love to learn and you love to work, who knows how far you will go? Just see what happened to a poor boy named Mike.

Uncle Arthur

Mike, the Blacksmith's Son

Mike was only a blacksmith's son. But he succeeded in giving to the world the secret of a great new power.

Mike was born in London, England, in 1791. That was just a few years after the Colonists in America had signed the Declaration of Independence. At that time, there were no phones, no radios, no TVs. There was not a single electric light, or motor, or anything else electrical in all the world.

As a boy, Mike played around his father's forge. No doubt he worked the big bellows that made the fire white-hot. Day after day he watched his father hammering the heated iron in the anvil. His father made horseshoes and metal rims for wooden coach wheels.

But Mike's family was poor, and he was thin and hungry. Often there was not enough to eat. All the money Father earned had to be used for food and clothing. So there was no money left for Mike's education. At 13 he left school and went to work.

 That meant no high school for him, and no university degree.

Fortunately, Mike longed for knowledge, and loved to read. More fortunate still, he was apprenticed to a bookbinder. All sorts of books came to the bindery to be bound. Mike read as many of them as he could, especially the scientific books. Some of these were about chemistry. Others were about electricity. He enjoyed them more than any storybook.

Eventually Mike began to do some of the experiments mentioned in these books. He even thought up some new ones by himself. He began to see that there were wonderful possibilities in electricity. How he wished to know more about these things! If only he could go to school and learn about them from a teacher!

One day a customer came into the bindery. He knew of Mike's interest in science. "Would you like to attend a lecture," said the customer, "by the famous scientist Sir Humphry Davy?" Mike did not need a second invitation.

That night was a turning point in the boy's life. He took full notes of everything the great scientist said. These he copied carefully and bound in a beautiful leather binding. He sent the notes to Sir Humphry with a letter telling of his deep interest in science.

Some time later, on December 24, 1812, there was a knock on Mike's door. It was a messenger from Sir Humphry Davy himself! The messenger invited Mike to come and see Sir Humphry the next day.

Talk about a "shot heard round the world"! That was a knock heard round the world. It was as if that visit turned on the lights in your house!

Soon after the visit, Mike left the bookbindery and went to work for the great scientist. He earned 25 shillings a week, a little more than $5. But he didn't care about wages; he loved his new job. He was happy beyond words.

Eagerly Mike watched Sir Humphry carry out his experiments. He kept careful note of every step. So pleased was the scientist with his new assistant that he took him along as a secretary when he went on a trip around Europe. On this trip Mike met many other scientists and made friends who were a great help to him later on.

Back in the London laboratory, Mike began to do more and more experiments, often with breathtaking results. It is said that Mike "worked out his problems for the sheer joy of solving them." That, perhaps, is why he did solve them.

Just 13 years after Mike joined the laboratory staff, Sir Humphry Davy retired. But before he left, the great scientist appointed Mike as the new director of the laboratory. Now Mike pressed on in his research with fresh zeal. Six years later he announced a major discovery—the principle of electromagnetism. Few peo-

From Mike's discovery came the electric motor, the great new power that was to light the world and run its machinery.

ple living then understood what it was all about. But from this discovery came the electric motor and the electric dynamo, the great new power that was to light the world and run its machinery.

If it hadn't been for Mike—Michael Faraday—we might never have had many of the comforts and conveniences we enjoy today. Just think how many wheels would stop, how many lights would go out, how many radios and TVs would go silent, if all the electric motors and dynamos in the world suddenly ceased to turn! We would realize then how much we owe to this blacksmith's son who became a scientist.

Some boys and girls today think that they cannot hope to do anything worthwhile in life. They think that they'll probably fail unless they have "pull" or special privileges, or unless someone gives them a lot of money. If you are one of these, remember Mike, the boy who had nothing on earth except the love of knowledge, and who worked hard enough to succeed. Those are the real secrets of success.

❖ Exploring the Story ❖

You can have a successful STORYTIME™ adventure by simply reading the story to your child. The activities below are optional additions to your adventure. Use an activity after the story is read, or save it for later. The grade levels may guide your choice, but select the activity your child will most enjoy.

Discussing the Story

Small beginnings can end up with big results. Can you think of any examples? There are many examples in nature, because every plant and animal starts out very small, doesn't it? Even you!

There are also many stories of how people in very humble circumstances eventually found their way into places where they could be of great service to the rest of the world. Helen Keller is a famous woman who traveled the world many times, giving lectures, writing books, and doing all she could to help the blind and deaf. Yet Helen Keller nearly grew up imprisoned in a body that could not hear or see.

It took another young woman, orphaned, home-less, and nearly blind herself, to find the key to Helen's world. The two of them together, with much courage, determination, and hard work, gave a great gift to humankind.

Do you feel like you are only a small beginning of what you would like to be? What is the best way to go about getting big results out of your life?

Fun Footnotes

What do you think of when you think of a magnet? You may think of a bar that attracts nails and paper clips. That is a magnet, to be sure. But you might be surprised to find out that a magnetic field surrounds our galaxy. A field a million times stronger than the magnetic field around our galaxy surrounds our earth. And fields a million times stronger than the field around our earth are inside atoms, pieces of our world so small no one has ever seen them, until recently (see the April 1989 issue of *Popular Science* for some of the first photographs of atoms).

Magnets work in generators to create electricity. Magnets in your telephone, radio, and TV sets change electricity into sound. Magnets are busy working all around you!

STORYTIME Fun Activities

Magnets (preschool)

Magnets make fun toys. You can explore the magnetic fields around bar magnets with a sheet of white paper and iron filings or bits of steel wool. Scatter the iron filings on the paper, and arrange the bars underneath the paper. Tap the paper lightly, and watch the pattern in which the filings line up.

Bring two bars end to end, and watch the filings. Switch ends. Line the bars up parallel with each other. Try

drawing pictures with one of the bars. Experiment with both ends of the bar. Does one end work better? Put some other objects under the paper with the magnets, such as a piece of coat hanger wire. Run a magnet along the steel wire several times, and see if the wire will attract filings.

Electromagnet (early elementary)

You can show that electricity can turn a nail into a magnet. You will need a four- to six-inch iron nail, insulated copper wire, and a six-volt battery. Wrap the wire about 100 times around the nail and connect the two ends to the battery. Now your iron nail is an electromagnet and will pick up other small iron objects.

Michael Faraday studied electromagnets and became convinced that since electricity could produce magnetism, magnetism should produce electricity. After much work, he finally proved that this was so.

Generator (later elementary)

You can show, like Faraday did, that a magnet can produce electricity. This is the principle that the electric generator is built on. First, make a simple galvanometer. A galvanometer indicates current. Place a magnetic compass on a block of wood just as wide as the compass and an inch or two longer.

Wrap about 12 feet of enameled copper wire in a neat coil around the block. Tie the coil together at several points with thread, and turn the coil on end over the compass, with the bottom of the coil under the block. Sand away the enamel on the two ends of the wire.

Wrap about 12 feet of wire into a coil large enough to slip over a permanent magnet. Connect the wires of the galvanometer to the coil, and move the coil back and forth over the magnet. The needle on the compass should move, showing that the coil moving over the magnet is producing electricity.

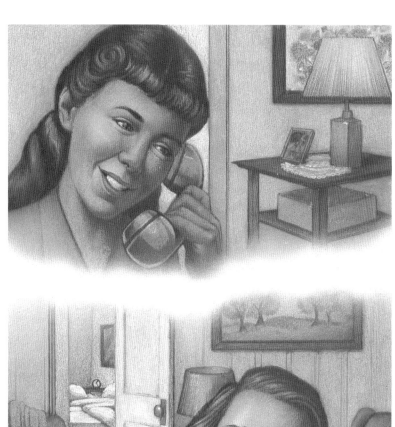

"You'll have to agree I may try my own plans for keeping order," said Aunt Mary.

Messy houses are hard to live in. It's hard to find things, and if you've ever tried to walk to the light switch in the dark when there are toys scattered all over your floor, you know what a trick that can be! There are many remedies for keeping order, though, as Aunt Mary showed the children and parents in this story.

Uncle Arthur

Aunt Mary's Remedy

The telephone rang several times before Aunt Mary picked it up.

It was her sister who was calling. "John has just heard that he must attend the university for the next six months, and I was wondering—"

"I know," interrupted Aunt Mary. "You were wondering if I would come over and look after those little rascals of yours while you go away with your husband. If that's it, the answer is no, thanks!"

"Oh, Mary, you don't mean that. They've promised they'll be really good this time. They'll keep the place tidier than you've ever seen it."

"I don't believe it," said Aunt Mary, who was very particular, and liked everything just so. "I can't live where everything is upside down and nobody can ever find anything. Before I come to look after your chil-

89

dren again, you will have to let me try my own plans."

"I agree, of course, Mary," her sister said, relief showing in her voice. "You may do anything you like. Only come. You know we couldn't do without you."

That was how Aunt Mary found herself in charge of her sister's four children for the next six months.

There were Laura, age 14; Ivan, 10; Diana, 8; and Julia, 2. It was no small responsibility, especially since none of them had been taught to be tidy or punctual. They did what they liked, and didn't mind how untidy the house became.

Aunt Mary looked at her problem carefully and wondered where to be-

gin. Then she decided that the best way to do what she wanted was to suggest a new game for all of them to play.

She called it the "Pocket Money Game."

The name captured the children's interest at once. Laura, Ivan, and Diana had never had pocket money before. Mother or Father handed out dimes and pennies only when they happened to think about it.

"From now on," said Aunt Mary, "you will have a certain stated allowance every week."

"When does it begin?" cried all three together.

"Today. This very afternoon."

"Hooray!" they cried.

"But just a minute," said Aunt Mary. "That isn't all of the game. The amount that you get each week will depend on the way you fill in these cards."

"What cards?" they asked.

Aunt Mary showed them. There was a card for each of them. Each one was carefully ruled, making a

90

number of little squares. Along the top were the days of the week: Sunday, Monday, Tuesday, and so on. Down the left-hand side was a list of certain things to be done daily, such as "Up before seven," "Breakfast on time," "Teeth brushed," "Clothes put away," "Clothes ready for the morning," "Prayers said," "Bible read," "In bed by eight."

"Now," said Aunt Mary, "for every day on which all of these items have a red check mark, you will get one seventh of your pocket money. If a check is missing, you will lose one seventh of it."

"Oh!" they said. "Then we won't get any at all."

"Oh, yes, you will," said Aunt Mary. "You may lose a day or two at first, but soon you will have perfect records, and get your money every week. But I haven't shown you all of the game yet."

Were they in for a surprise!

On the sideboard in the dining room was a small card: "One penny fine for anything left on me."

Near the sink in the kitchen was a similar notice.

In Father's study, there was another notice. It said, "One penny fine if you don't leave me clean and tidy."

The children laughed, but soon became serious.

"We'll lose all we get," said Ivan. "We won't have a penny to our names," said Laura and Diana.

"Who's going to collect the fines?" asked Ivan.

"Ah, now we come to the other part of the game," said Aunt Mary. "All the fines will be put into a box on the dining room table. Then, once a week, everything in the box will go to the one who has the

ONE PENNY
FINE FOR
ANYTHING
LEFT ON ME

*What excitement there was as the children waited to
find out who had won.*

highest number of red checks on his card."

"Oh, that's great!" cried Ivan. "That means me! I'm
going to get that boxful every time."

"No, you're not," said the girls. "We are."

Aunt Mary laughed. "Of course, there may not be
much in it," she said, "if you all remember to do everything right all the time."

So the children began the game. What fun they
had! They watched each other. And they watched the
check marks on the cards as Aunt Mary carefully put
them on (or left them off) each night! Pretty soon the
fines began to jingle in the box on the dining room
table. Laura left her hairbrush on the drainboard. Ivan
left his tie clip on the bathroom shelf. Laura forgot
she had dropped bits of paper all over the study floor.

What excitement there was when the red checks
were counted for the first time! None of the children
had full marks. One had got up late two or three

times. Another had failed to brush his teeth. Another had forgotten to say his prayers. Oh, how easy it was to lose points! And how hard to get a perfect record!

When the fine box was opened, it contained 26 cents! It all went to Laura because she had the highest marks. The other two were disappointed, but they made up their minds to try harder next week.

Next week they did better. The next, better still.

One week Ivan actually got a red check in every space on his card, so the money in the fine box was his. But this time it wasn't as much as usual, for all were remembering better now. They didn't leave things around as they used to do.

When Mother and Father came home, what a difference they noticed! How neat everything was!

"Aunt Mary!" they exclaimed. "What have you done? It's wonderful!"

Then something happened.

Father left his hammer on the drainboard, and was promptly fined! Mother left a curler on the bathroom shelf, and her penny was collected too. It was a shock at first, but they paid up and entered into the fun.

For a while the fine box got quite heavy again, and it was always one of the children who won the pennies in it. Pretty soon, Father and Mother caught on, and gave them a run for their money.

By that time the place had become so neat and orderly, it was like a brand-new house. From a muddle madhouse, it had become a beautiful, peaceful home. Aunt Mary's remedy had worked!

You can have a successful STORYTIME™ adventure by simply reading the story to your child. The activities below are optional additions to your adventure. Use an activity after the story is read, or save it for later. The grade levels may guide your choice, but select the activity your child will most enjoy.

Discussing the Story

Keeping a house clean is sometimes difficult, but it's a different kind of difficult than vaulting a 10-foot pole, for instance. Why do you think keeping a place clean is hard for some people?

Are there any habits your family has that make it hard for you to keep your house clean? Write down these habits. Now decide how you can make new habits that will make housecleaning easier. Work on one at a time, and reward the whole family for learning a new habit.

Take the habit of hanging up coats as an example. Make sure there is a place for each person to hang up his coat. Mark on a sheet of paper each time someone must be reminded to hang up a coat. When your family goes for a whole week with three or less marks, go out for pizza or some other activity the entire family will enjoy!

Fun Footnotes

The word *habit* comes from the Latin word *habitus*. Like many words, habit has different meanings. Habit could mean a costume worn for certain occasions, such as a riding habit worn to ride horses. Habit can also mean a tendency to perform a certain action or behave in a certain way. It also describes the tendency of a plant or animal to grow in a certain way. See if you can write sentences using the word *habit* with each of these meanings.

STORYTIME Fun Activities

Sweeping (preschool)

To do a good job sweeping, you will need a broom just your size. Buy a lightweight broom at the grocery store. The broom should stand just a bit shorter than you are. You may need to cut off a too-long broomstick with a saw, sanding the rough edges.

To make your broom even more special, take one of your smaller stuffed animals that you don't mind cutting a bit. Snip a hole in the top and the bottom of the back of the toy, and work a hole through the stuffing with a screwdriver. Slip your stuffed pet over the handle of the broom and push it down low on the broomstick. Now you both are ready to sweep!

Start in one corner of a room, and sweep all the way across the end of the room. Sweep with low, easy swings, so the dirt you are sweeping up doesn't fly through the air. When you get to the end of the room, step back several feet into the room, and sweep your way back across. Your mother will love to have your help keeping the kitchen floor clean!

Pajama Bag (early elementary)

Could you use a special place to put your pajamas? A pajama bag is fun and easy to make. Put a wad of stuffing down one side of the bottom of an old pillowcase. Pull a man's white sport sock over the wad. Then adjust the stuffing to make a head 12 to 14 inches around. Wrap the bottom of the head with string, and knot it.

To make arms, cut the rest of the sock in half by making a cut up to just below the doll's head, and another cut up the opposite side. Sew each strip together for each arm, stuff, and sew the ends to the pillowcase where the shoulders should be.

To make a baby doll pajama bag, put an old baby bonnet over

the head. Make a clown head by sewing on tufts of red or purple nylon netting (the kind that bunches of grapes are sold in) or yarn for hair. Sew on buttons for eyes, and use acrylic paint or clown makeup to make a mouth.

Gather a 3″ x 18″ strip of felt or lace down the center for a ruffle for the neck of your clown or doll. Decorate the rest of the pillowcase in any design you like. Make a hem at the bottom of the bag and insert a piece of elastic so it will hold your pajamas.

Catch-It-All Net (later elementary)

You can use this net to hold sports equipment, stuffed animals, or other bulky items. You will need 16 nylon cords each 6 feet long, and two brass rings. Tie the cords by twos on a rod of some kind placed on a wall where the cords will just touch the floor. A drapery rod might work well for you.

Tie your first row of knots 8 inches below the end of each cord. (Measure this before you tie up the cords.) Use a simple overhand knot, and tie the strands in the diamond pattern shown below. Keep the rows 4 to 5 inches apart.

Make your last row about 8 inches from the end of the cords. Tie the loose ends to a brass ring. Untie the cords at the top of the net, and tie them onto the other ring. Hang up your net in a closet or corner of your room, and fill!

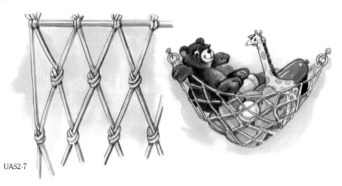

*Then Alan saw the package. It was small, about the size of
a sandwich, and wrapped in cellophane.*

*Honesty always pays. I don't mean that it always pays
money; many honest deeds are never known by anyone else on
earth. But an honest heart will pay far more than money. It will
make your life easier, make you a person of character respected
by all those around you, and will help prepare you to do important work in the world.*

Uncle Arthur

Alan's Sandwich

It was a beautiful summer
morning when 6-year-old Alan walked into one of the
lovely parks in the city where he lived. But Alan wasn't
thinking about the park. All he could think about was
that he was hungry. He wished he had brought some
lunch with him, at least an apple or a few cookies. He
searched his pockets, but couldn't find a crumb.

Then he saw the package. It was small, about the
size of a sandwich, and wrapped in cellophane. Feeling sure it must be a sandwich, he picked it up, hoping ants hadn't gotten inside and spoiled it.

It looked like a sandwich through the cellophane.
It was green inside, and you couldn't blame a hungry
boy for thinking it was something to eat. But it wasn't
a sandwich. It was money. Lots of money! Alan had
never seen so much money before in all his life.

In his excitement he forgot all about being hungry,

but he was puzzled as to what to do next.

His first thought was to run home and show his mother what he had found. Then he remembered something she had told him some time before.

"If you ever find anything that does not belong to you," she had said, "take it to a police station at once. The owner will probably be looking for it and will be very glad to get it back again. This will be doing to others as you would like them to do to you."

Alan thought about that a moment. He made up his mind. Putting the package in his pocket, he ran to the police station, which was not very far from the park gates. He pushed open the big glass door, then hesitated.

"What can I do for you, sonny?" asked the big policeman at the desk.

"Please, sir, I found something," said Alan. "It looks like money."

The policeman took the package.

"Whew!" he whistled as he counted out $210. "It surely is money. Where did you find this?"

Alan told his story.

"Thank you," said the policeman. "Thank you very much. We like honest boys such as you. We will keep the package here a few weeks and see if anybody claims it. If nobody does, we'll give it back to you."

"To me?" cried Alan excitedly.

"That's the law," said the policeman. "But don't get your hopes up too high. Usually people who lose a large amount of money soon begin asking for it.

Give me your name and address."

Alan ran home to tell his mother what had happened.

"I'm proud of you," she said. "You did exactly the right thing. Probably you won't get the money. You may not even get a reward for finding it. But never mind. You did what was honest and good, and that's what matters most."

Days, weeks, and months slipped by. Alan forgot all about his "sandwich." He also forgot about the hope that there might be a reward for finding the money.

October passed. So did November, and most of December. Only three days remained before Christmas. Mother should have been feeling very happy, but she wasn't. She had hoped so much that she might make this the best Christmas ever for her family. Now she knew she couldn't. There had been just too many bills to pay.

Suddenly there was a knock at the front door.

Mother hurried to open the door. Alan was not far behind her.

They were startled to see a big policeman outside.

"Whatever is the matter?" Mother asked anxiously.

"Nothing really, ma'am," he said kindly. "I believe you have a very honest little boy here."

"I hope so," she said. "You mean my Alan?"

"Yes," he said, producing a package from his pocket. "Some months ago he found this in the park

101

Mother was startled to see a big policeman outside. "Whatever is the matter?" she asked anxiously.

and brought it to the police station."

"It's my 'sandwich'!" Alan yelled with delight.

"Well," said the policeman, "since nobody has claimed it, we will give it to the finder. Please sign this receipt."

Mother signed, and the policeman went on his way. What shouts of joy filled the house!

Alan and Mother used part of the money to open a savings account for Alan. With another part they bought some much needed clothes. And part of the money they spent to get everybody some extra special gifts for Christmas. Alan's "sandwich" proved to be filled with Christmas cheer.

❖ Exploring the Story ❖

You can have a successful STORYTIME™ adventure by simply reading the story to your child. The activities below are optional additions to your adventure. Use an activity after the story is read, or save it for later. The grade levels may guide your choice, but select the activity your child will most enjoy.

Discussing the Story

How would you describe an honest person? First make a list of what an honest person does do, then make a list of what an honest person doesn't do. You will probably include in your first list that an honest person tells the truth. In your second list, you might mention that he or she doesn't lie or steal. What else is on your list?

Do you feel like an honest person makes a good friend?

Fun Footnotes

The motto "In God We Trust" first appeared on United States coins in 1864, but it wasn't until 1955 that Congress passed a law that all U.S. coins should have this motto.

STORYTIME Fun Activities

Drawing an Apple (preschool)

You will want to learn to say this poem and draw the picture, too. Read the poem slowly as you draw the picture, step by step. Practice it several times, and share it with your friends.

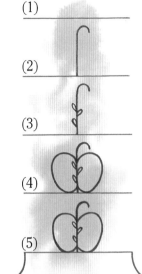

Here lies a piece of earth, (1)

And here sprouts a baby tree, (2)

Help me count the tiny leaves:

One, two, three. (3)

When we draw around it

With a curl and a bump, (4)

You see half an apple,

Sitting on a stump. (5)

Going Shopping (early elementary)

Lay out some small toys, books, or other items on a table. Put tags on each item, such as "28 cents," "44 cents," and so on. Lay out coins in rows on the table. You should have several rows of pennies, a row of nickels, another of dimes, and one of quarters. Take turns "buying" items, using the coins in front of you, until the money runs out.

A variation of this game can be used as a reward for accomplishing certain tasks in the house. For example, for each chore accomplished the person receives a check mark. Someone who earns 36 check

marks during the week for certain household chores may be able to exchange the check marks for 36 cents, with which he can buy individual stickers, beads, small bells, shells, or other inexpensive items arranged and tagged in a "store" somewhere in your home.

Money Portraits (later elementary)

Find as many different kinds of U.S. coins as you can. You should have a penny, a nickel, a dime, a quarter, maybe even a half dollar or a dollar. Put a sheet of paper over each coin, color it with a crayon, to get a print. You can make play money this way.

Can you identify who or what is on each side of the coins? What do each of the men on the coins have in common? Can you arrange the coins in order by which president served first, second, etc.?

See if you can identify the portraits on paper dollars.

*Sylvia began to get more and more worried as the doctor
continued to test her eyes.*

Sometimes people make up their minds they don't like some-thing, even though they really don't know all the facts about it. Have you ever looked at a dish of food and said you didn't like it without even tasting it? Sylvia had this problem, but it wasn't food that was bothering her.

Uncle Arthur

Sylvia's Glasses

If there was one thing Sylvia hoped she would never have to do, it was to wear glasses. She thought that glasses spoiled girls' looks and made them plain and homely. When she looked in the mirror at her own pretty features, she often thought that to have to wear glasses would be the worst thing that could happen to her.

One day the blow fell. All joy vanished from her life. Sylvia thought she could never be happy again. Teacher had sent her home from school with a note saying that she should have her eyes tested. She was holding her books too close to her face!

"Don't look so worried," said Mother after she had read the note. "It isn't any trouble to have one's eyes tested, and it doesn't hurt."

"But Mother," cried Sylvia, "you don't think I'll

have to wear glasses, do you? I couldn't. I simply couldn't."

"Well, we don't know, do we?" said Mother. "Let's go find out. That's the wise thing to do."

So off they went to an optometrist, a doctor who tested Sylvia's eyes. There were all kinds of wonderful instruments in the doctor's office. Sylvia had to admit that the test didn't hurt at all. She began to get more and more worried, however, as the doctor continued to put little pieces of glass in front of her eyes, asking whether she could see better with this or that.

She had hoped that he would tell her that her eyes were perfectly all right. Or that they were just a little tired. Or that they needed only a short rest. Now here he was trying glasses on her eyes as though she had to have them anyway!

When the examination was completed, the doctor turned to Mother and broke the news. "She certainly does need glasses," he said, "and she should have had them some time ago. I can have them ready for her in about 10 days, if that will be all right."

Mother agreed, and they left the doctor's office. Sylvia trailed behind, her face red with anger.

"I won't wear them, Mother. I won't, I tell you!"

"But Sylvia, you need them," said Mother gently. "They will help you so much. I believe you will be able to learn your lessons easier, and maybe you won't get so many headaches."

"I don't care!" said Sylvia. "I'd rather have head-aches than wear nasty old glasses. They will make me look so old and homely."

"Oh, you shouldn't be thinking about that," said Mother, smiling. "Your health is far more important than your looks. Anyway, I think you'll look all right in glasses, Sylvia."

For many years lenses were ground, fitted in frames, and sold on the street. The buyer selected the pair that suited him.

But Sylvia was not to be comforted. She had made up her mind that she was going to hate glasses, that she wouldn't wear them, and that was that.

"I wish I could get hold of the person who invented glasses!" she said bitterly. "I'd—I'd—"

"That would be rather difficult," said Mother. "You would have to travel a long, long way. Hundreds of miles and hundreds of years. The Chinese are supposed to be the first to have worn them. Their great hero Confucius tells in his writings how he gave a pair to a poor cobbler. That was about 500 B.C. Another story from China tells of a rich man who gave one of his finest horses for a pair of glasses around A.D. 1260. But those glasses may have been just ornaments."

"Ornaments!" snorted Sylvia. "Fancy wearing the horrid things as ornaments!"

109

"Oh, many people have done that," said Mother. "But usually, of course, they are worn only as a help to the eyes. The man who gets the credit for this idea is Roger Bacon, who wrote about them in A.D. 1276. He said eyeglasses were useful to those 'who are old and have weak sight.' "

"But I'm not old," said Sylvia.

"Not very," smiled Mother, "though evidently, you do have weak sight. But let me finish the story of glasses. The first maker of them in Europe is believed to have been an Italian called Salvino D'Armato of Florence. We know this because of the words on his tombstone in one of the old churches in that city: 'Here lies Salvino D'Armato, of the Amati of Florence. Inventor of Spectacles. God pardon him for his sins. A.D. 1317.' "

"His sins?" asked Sylvia. "Making spectacles, maybe."

"No," said Mother, laughing. "That wasn't one of his sins. His work proved a great blessing to many people. For many years after that, spectaclemaking was a trade, like shoemaking or carpentry. Lenses were ground, fitted in frames, and sold on the streets. The buyer selected the pair that suited him. There were no optometrists then to test people's eyes as yours were tested."

Slowly the 10 days went by. All the time Sylvia worried about how she would look in her glasses. When they arrived, Sylvia nervously slipped them on. At once she noticed how clear everything was all about her. She picked up a book and saw how easy it was to read.

"Why Mother," she said, "these things make everything different. All the world seems new!"

And the world was new—to her. She had never

*When Sylvia finally looked in the mirror, she had
another big surprise.*

seen it properly before. She had not realized what a
burden she was carrying, nor what darkness she had
been living in so long.

So thrilled was Sylvia at the clear vision she now
had that she actually forgot to look in the mirror. That
is, for an hour or two. When she did look, she had
another surprise.

"Why!" she exclaimed, "I don't look so bad in
them after all!"

You can have a successful STORYTIME™ adventure by simply reading the story to your child. The activities below are optional additions to your adventure. Use an activity after the story is read, or save it for later. The grade levels may guide your choice, but select the activity your child will most enjoy.

Discussing the Story

Is there anything about your looks you'd like to change? Most of us have something about ourselves we wish were different. We have to put up with glasses, or straight hair, or skinny legs, when we'd rather have more say in how we look. You'll be happiest if you learn to make the best of what you have.

Remember, you aren't the only one. Many kids worry that everyone is staring at them, when really, almost everybody else is worried about his own ears, or feet, or freckles. What you feel about yourself is similar to what many others feel about themselves. If you remember this, you can be more understanding and accepting of yourself, and of others.

Think of the bright side. Perhaps you have some points that you don't think are good (which no one else may have even noticed!), but you probably have some very attractive features, too. Thinking of these nice points about yourself will give you confidence when you are with others.

Fun Footnotes

A hologram is a 3-D picture that is flat, but doesn't look like it. You don't need to use special glasses to see holograms. The December 1988 issue of *National Geographic* has a hologram on the front cover. You should be able to find it in your library.

STORYTIME Fun Activities

Seeing in the Dark (preschool)

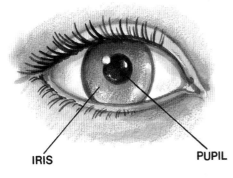

IRIS   PUPIL

Look at your eyes in the mirror. Do you see the black circle in the middle of your eye? That is called the pupil. The pupil is a hole where light can go through to the inside of your eye. The hole is covered by a special see-through covering that lets the light in, but keeps dust and dirt out.

Your pupil can get bigger to let more light in when it is dark, or smaller when there is plenty of light. Turn off the light, and wait for your eyes to get used to the dark. Use a flashlight to look at your pupils in the mirror. Did they get bigger?

Seeing in Stereo (early elementary)

Did you ever wonder why you have two eyes? Being able to see two pictures of the same thing from a little different perspective—one picture from your right eye, and another from your left eye—helps your brain measure depth better.

Try this experiment. Ask someone to hold a pencil straight up and down, about two feet in front of you. Close one eye, and hold one arm straight out beside you. Slowly bring your arm around in front of you, and try to touch the tip of the pencil with the tip of your finger. Try this several times, and then open both eyes, and try it again.

Upside-down Pictures (later elementary)

You can make a slide projector by 1) cutting a hole in a box, 2) taping a piece of aluminum foil over the hole, 3) making a small pinhole in the foil, 4) taping the slide in front of the light source (flashlight), and 5) putting the light inside the box. You will probably see a fuzzy picture shining upside down on the wall in front of the box.

How would you make the picture right side up? You have to tape the slide upside down! Did you know that the images reflected on the back of your eye are upside-down, too? Your brain interprets the images as right side up, so you see things properly.

To understand why the images on your eye are upside-down, remember that light travels in straight lines. It doesn't bend. Let's use the image from the slide as an example. As the light from the bulb passes through the slide, the light that is coming from the top of the picture goes in a straight line to the bottom of the image on the wall. The light that goes through the bottom of the slide ends up at the top of the image on the wall, and so the image looks upside-down.

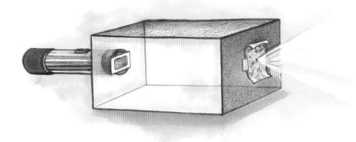

PART THREE

THE STORYGUIDE™ SECTION

MOTIVATING YOUR CHILD

Your son is sitting at the piano picking out the tune to "Jingle Bells." He's bright, and has a good ear. His piano teacher says he could become a concert pianist if he wanted to. You just don't know how to get him to practice, instead of playing around with simple tunes.

Your daughter has a charming smile, but she whines. You've done everything you can to stop the habit. But you can't seem to help her see what a bad habit her whining is.

And so the list goes. How do you get your children to keep their rooms clean? How do you get them to eat what's put in front of them? How do you get them to *want* to do well in school?

Most parents have strong feelings about what constitutes acceptable behavior. We soon learn, however, that it is one thing for us to feel this way, and quite another to get our children to feel the same way we do. That's where motivation comes in. External (outside) motivation is what you use to get children to do what needs to be done. Internal (inside) motivation is what gets children to *want* to do what needs to be done.

What Motivates the Young Child

Let's examine the principles of motivation.

1. We are motivated by the hope of reward.

Every good behavior has a reward. Your hard work

is rewarded with a paycheck. Pleasing manners mean more friends. But the rewards may be more obvious to you than to your child. Sometimes the benefits are too abstract or too far down the road for a young child to readily understand.

So when motivating young children through rewards, it helps to offer benefits they can readily understand. For example, a daily reward of a check mark or sticker on a chart for keeping his room clean is a positive way of getting a child in the habit of making his bed and picking up after himself.

2. We can be motivated by fear of punishment.

When we must motivate the very young child to stay out of the street or obey some other safety rule, we need absolute, complete obedience. Sometimes, when other options don't work, it is necessary to use punishment to motivate our children. (The general merits of discipline are discussed further in volume 3 of the STORYGUIDE section, but they should be recognized here as a motivation option.)

3. Natural consequences are excellent motivators.

You call your child to get ready to go with a neighbor family to the zoo, but the youngster dallies. You could scold, threaten, and hurry the child along, but in doing so you would sacrifice the peace and quiet of the home. It is much more effective to calmly say one time, "If you are ready when they arrive, you may go to the zoo with them. If you're late, they'll have to leave without you." Few children will need more than one missed trip to understand the connection between their actions and the reward.

4. Questions and discussions motivate better than commands and demands.

Children learn best when they feel they have a voice in what's happening. As early as possible, ask for your child's input in family affairs. As your children grow old enough to question your reasoning, encourage those questions. Use questions of your own, as well as discussions, to help your children understand the reasons behind the requests you make of them.

The youthful members of one family couldn't understand why they always had to tell their parents where they were going, and when they would return. At their urging, the rule was removed. A few days later the children came home from school to discover that mother was nowhere about. No one knew where she had gone, or when she would return. The children waited many anxious hours for mom to get back. When she finally came home, they couldn't help asking where she had gone, and why she hadn't let them know when she would be back. They soon agreed that the old rule wasn't such a bad idea after all!

Motivations That Work From the Inside Out

As children grow older and learn to reason, we must wean them from a dependency on external motivators and help them switch to the more powerful force of internal motivation. Motivation that comes from within the child. How can you help your child form this internal motivation? Here are a few pointers.

1. Your child wants to become what you are.

Since you, as parents, are in the spotlight of your child's world, you are the primary examples of all your child wants to become. He wants to be what you are. He learns to value what you value. He learns to treat others the way you treat him and others. That's why you need to be what you want your child to be.[1]

2. Your child wants to do well when he likes him-

self, and believes he can do well.

One of the most important values your child absorbs from you is your value of him as a person. Your child needs to feel that he is important to the people who matter to him. He needs to feel he can do well in something that is important to him. He needs to feel he can make some important decisions in his own life. He also needs to do what is right, in order to think well of himself.[2] You can help your child reach these goals by accepting him as a person of worth,

---

When your child feels good about who he is, he is more likely to try new things and test his abilities.

---

always worthy of your love. Assure him that your love is unconditional, even when his behavior is not always the best. Encourage him to meet the standards your family has set, rather than condemn his failures. Let him know when he has done well, and reward him with more decision-making power when he has demonstrated that he can make wise choices.

When your child feels good about who he is, he is more likely to try new things and test his abilities. Failures will not put him down for long, because they will not hurt his basic view of his worth as a person. He believes that eventually he will succeed, because you believe he can.

3. Your child wants to achieve when he has experienced success.

Success breeds success. Watch a child try to manipulate a light switch. As soon as he realizes he is capable of moving the switch, he is eager to try all the other switches in the house. He learns to be confident in his ability to manipulate gadgets.

You can help a child develop this confidence in his own abilities by monitoring his attempts at doing things. Allow him a fair, full chance at solving his problems. But be sensitive enough to tell when a job looks doomed to frustration and failure, and step in just enough to boost him over the frustrating part. Don't allow your child to lose his initiative because of impossible tasks, or to get into the habit of only half finishing a job.

Give your child a chance to excel at something. As your child discovers what he is good at doing and what he wants to be good at doing, which is not always the same thing, give him your support. This may mean extra evenings at the pool, or an investment in music lessons. It should always mean encouragement. In the difficult world of school and peer pressure, your child's skills can give him an edge that will help him preserve his self-concept and dignity and provide him with the ability to resist peer pressure.

4. Your child wants to branch out into new fields when he has had success in trying new things.

Sometimes simply exposing your child to something new is all you need to do to interest him. If it happens to be an area in which you have little or no interest, put aside any of your own prior knowledge of the subject or feelings of prejudice that might be in the way. Then, as you help your child learn, both of you will discover fascinating subjects you may have once thought were not worth exploring.

You can use the principle of moving from the known to the unknown in introducing new material. For example, if your child is interested in snakes but could care less about geography, introduce geography by plotting the habitats of snakes around the world. As your child achieves success in new areas, he will become more motivated to step out into other untried fields of investigation. He will learn from experience that he can have fun and success in nearly everything he does.

5. Your child wants to accomplish great things when he learns about other people who have accomplished great things.

Along with the new subject matter you introduce to your child, introduce new role models. Find people in your community and in books who can inspire your child to achieve in new areas.

Biblical heroes and heroines, true stories of children who successfully face the same temptations as your own child, can all serve as excellent role models. They can also help motivate your child to develop positive character traits.

EXTENDING
YOUR CHILD'S HORIZONS

The mind is a fascinating treasure, and each one is unique. As you begin to get acquainted with the budding person within each of your children, you will want to search for clues that help you understand how to reach each child's imagination, what makes him excited, what touches his emotions.

Discovering what interests a child is like discovering the key to that child's mind. Discovering how a child learns best is like discovering how the key turns. As you work with your child, the two of you will find the unique gifts your child possesses. How should you go about helping your child develop his potential?

Introduce Your Child
to Character-building Values

By your example, and by the example of others who figure in the stories you read to your child, you illustrate to your child the principles by which he will build his life. In these experiences, your child learns what is important in life. Is ambition important? Is it more important than compassion and honesty? What are the goals in life to strive for? Is family contentment and security more or less important than money? What is the proper way to gain success?

These questions deserve the most careful attention. Your child's understanding of the answers to these and similar questions plays a major part in directing the course of your child's future decisions.

Character is the foundation of a secure, happy, productive life. But your child will need other information, too.

Introduce Your Child
to the World Around Him

You will want to give your child knowledge and experience about the world he lives in.

1. Introduce science.

Have you ever seen a toddler hover about the door, hoping for a chance to go outside? What does he do when he gets there? He heads straight for dirt and rocks and water puddles! You will enjoy sharing his experiences as he meets the sun and the stars, the wind and the rain, the flowers, the birds, and everything else that stirs in the great outdoors.

Nature is your child's first textbook. Let him play freely with all that he can safely handle in the outdoors. He won't be able to soak up enough of it. There does come a time for books, but let them back up what your child learns firsthand, wherever possible.

2. Introduce the arts of communication.

As your child's interests and understanding grow, read him poetry about what he loves best. Read poetry and listen to the rhythm of the language. When your child learns to love stories, talk about the people in the stories, until they become real to your child. What kinds of feelings did they seem to have? What ways did they react to certain situations? Let your child talk about how he is like the characters in the stories and how he is different.

Children love water, paint, mud, and clay. They are messy, to be sure. But they're also an invaluable means of letting your child explore what he can do, creating an idea out of a shapeless mass.

3. Introduce geography.

Start with a simple map of your child's room. Then draw a map of the entire house. Keep maps of the world, the United States, and your state around the house and handy. Use them often yourself, and your child will become curious about them. He'll want to know where his home is located on the map. He will ask where his grandparents live, where he traveled to on a vacation. When he reads the story of an African child, he will want to see where Africa is. When he notices the label on a toy that says "Made in China," help him search for China on the globe. Soon geography will become part of your child's everyday experience.

4. Introduce history.

Acquaint your child with the people behind the inventions of the airplane, the telephone, the light bulb. Read about scientists who overcame great obstacles to make the advances we have today. As your child learns more and more of history, he will better understand the role he can play in life's events.

Games, Crafts, and Experiments

One of the best ways to reach a child's imagination is to use the same methods the child uses to have fun. Children love games. The goals are obvious, the rules are spelled out, the results of their actions are immediate, and they love to win! Games can motivate your children to learn everything from keeping a house straight to math—while they are having fun.

Often children feel that what they are learning has nothing to do with their everyday needs and lives.

While children do need to learn to work for the future rather than simply live for the moment, try to make much of what your children learn profitable right away. For example, if they make a map of the community, find a way to make the map available to visitors or new residents.

Arts and crafts introduce your child to numerous ways of putting things together and getting things

To help your child get the most out of life, encourage learning and working habits that will help him enjoy life.

done. They help children use problem-solving skills in everyday situations. Crafts are also a good introduction to goal setting. You can help your child learn to set goals in terms of what he wants to get done, how long it should take him, and how he expects to accomplish his task. Children don't understand why crafts are good for them; they just think they are having a good time!

Experiments are simply ways of looking at the world around us. You can start off with walks. Look, see, smell, listen, and touch. Add nets, collection bags and bottles, magnifying glasses. Then read about and discuss what you and your children find. Try listing everything you find in a square foot of backyard, a rotten stump, or pond water. Then check the same spot over the seasons and note any changes. Experiment and have fun!

To help your child get the most out of life, encourage learning and working habits that will help him enjoy life.

An experiment conducted in a medical research

institution tested the effects of exercise on reducing cholesterol levels, with interesting results. Those who enjoyed running on the treadmill succeeded in lowering their cholesterol. Those who ran the treadmill just as much but didn't enjoy running not only failed in lowering their cholesterol count, but in some cases actually raised it! It pays to enjoy what we do.

Nearly everything in our world brings pleasure at the same time that it is useful. Leaves, butterflies, and clouds are beautiful, yet leaves manufacture oxygen and food, butterflies pollinate plants, and clouds bear moisture. We must eat to live, but what we eat is tasty. We sleep so our bodies can rebuild themselves, but sleeping is a pleasure. Show your child that life is a delight, but its purpose is to use the gifts we have to help others.

As you plan games, crafts, and experiments, and as you help your child become familiar with the stimulating variety of the world around him, the biggest benefits come not only from the facts your child learns from his lessons, but from the attitudes he develops out of all your activities.

In the process of learning and doing a wide variety of things, your child will discover what it is he enjoys most, what he is best at, and what others appreciate most about him. This knowledge will help your child find his place in life where he can do the most good, and enjoy becoming all he can be.

----

[1] Elizabeth B. Murlock, *Adolescent Development* (New York: McGraw-Hill, 1973), p. 376.

[2] Harold Bernard, *Human Development in Western Culture,* 5th ed. (Boston: Allyn & Bacon, 1978), p. 399.